Child-Initiated Play and Learning

Child-Initiated Play and Learning shows how a creative approach to learning that allows for spontaneous adventures in play through child-led projects can lead to rich learning experiences that build on children's own interests. This second edition has been fully updated in light of policy and curriculum changes and features new material to help practitioners make informed decisions around digital technology and how children engage with it.

Including scenarios and provocative questions for reflective practice, this book looks at planning and considers the possibilities that should be encouraged when playing alongside young children. Drawing on practice from Reggio Emilia, New Zealand, Scandinavia and in settings in the UK, the book covers all aspects of planning including:

- how to enable and empower children to lead projects;
- organisation of indoor and outdoor materials and space;
- inclusive practice and contemporary research;
- learning through managing risks and adventurous play;
- working with parents and carers;
- challenging teams to explore what they actually believe about possibilities of play.

In a busy setting it can be difficult to adopt a flexible, creative approach to planning that embraces the unexpected rather than relying on templates or existing schemes of work. This book will give readers the confidence to adopt a flexible approach to planning that will better meet the needs of the children in their care.

The authors are experienced lecturers, practitioners, advisors and managers. Working with students, visiting placements, training teachers and early years professionals, they provide a sense of real purpose in their optimistic writing and enjoyment in the themes made explicit throughout this book.

Annie Woods has recently retired from Nottingham Trent University where she held a number of roles as an early years lecturer, programme leader and academic team leader. She developed a number of programmes and routes to early years qualifications and has been an external examiner in three universities. Prior to working in higher education, Annie taught in foundation stage and has been an assistant head teacher.

Child-Initiated Play and Learning

Planning for possibilities in the early years

SECOND EDITION

Edited by Annie Woods

Routledge
Taylor & Francis Group

LONDON AND NEW YORK

Second edition published 2017
by Routledge
2 Park Square, Milton Park, Abingdon, Oxon OX14 4RN

and by Routledge
711 Third Avenue, New York, NY 10017

Routledge is an imprint of the Taylor & Francis Group, an informa business

© 2017 A. Woods

First edition published 2013 by Routledge

British Library Cataloguing in Publication Data
A catalogue record for this book is available from the British Library

Library of Congress Cataloging in Publication Data
Names: Woods, Annie, editor of compilation.
Title: Child-initiated play and learning : planning for possibilities in the early years /
[edited by] Annie Woods.
Description: 2nd Edition. | New York : Routledge, 2017.
Identifiers: LCCN 2016035784 (print) | LCCN 2016037026 (ebook) |
ISBN 9781138688186 (hbk : alk. paper) | ISBN 9781138688193 (pbk : alk. paper) |
ISBN 9781315541969 (ebk)
Subjects: LCSH: Lesson planning. | Early childhood education.
Classification: LCC LB1027.4 .C53 2017 (print) | LCC LB1027.4 (ebook) |
DDC 372.21—dc23
LC record available at https://lccn.loc.gov/2016035784

ISBN: 978-1-138-68818-6 (hbk)
ISBN: 978-1-138-68819-3 (pbk)
ISBN: 978-1-315-54196-9 (ebk)

Typeset in Bembo
by Florence Production Ltd, Stoodleigh, Devon, UK

Contents

Contributors

Victoria Brown has worked at Nottingham Trent University as a senior and principal lecturer in primary and early years education for the past ten years. She has made the decision to return to her roots as a classroom teacher and embrace a move to Cornwall.

Catherine Gripton was a teacher in Nottingham and Nottinghamshire primary schools for fourteen years, teaching children across the 3–7 age range and becoming an Advanced Skills Teacher in 2003. Since 2008 she has worked as a senior lecturer in primary and early years initial teacher education at Nottingham Trent University.

Val Hall has worked as a senior lecturer in childhood studies at Nottingham Trent University. She has extensive experience as a special education teacher and senior manager within mainstream and generic special schools and as a local authority advisory teacher for autism and behaviour.

Cyndy Hawkins is Learning and Teaching Consultant and Fellow of the Higher Education Academy. She previously worked as a senior lecturer in childhood studies at Nottingham Trent University. Her academic background is in education, law and social sciences. She has worked as an early years practitioner and has taught in further and higher education on childhood studies related courses. Cyndy's research interests include children as consumers, children and risk society, and children and the media. She has published and presented at a number of international and national conferences and is the editor of *Rethinking Children as Consumers* and is a co-author for *Child-Initiated Play and Learning* and *Developing Inquiry for Learning* all Routledge.

Vicky McEwan has held a number of early years teaching roles before making the transition into advisory work. She worked as an early years advisor in Northamptonshire for many years supporting both schools and settings in the private, voluntary and independent sectors where she led on a range of initiatives, including under threes and working with parents and carers. Vicky is a lecturer at Nottingham Trent University where she initially led on the early years strand of a joint honours in education programme and currently works on the primary education programmes. Vicky is a trained forest school leader and is currently an early years governor at her local school.

Moira Moran taught in and led teams in nursery units and schools for more than twenty years, first in London then in Nottingham. She subsequently joined a team of Local Authority Early Years Specialist Teachers supporting practitioners in the PVI sector and teachers in school foundation units. She was involved with the Early Years Professional Status from its inception, as lecturer, mentor and assessor. Now at Nottingham Trent University, she lectures on the childhood studies and PGCE Early Years Initial Teacher Training courses. Her research areas are early play and the possibilities of the outdoors as an environment for young children's development. She is a forest school trainer.

Lorna Wardle has wealth of experience as an early years practitioner in schools and nurseries and has been a manager, trainer and local authority advisor in the PVCI sector. Lorna is now a senior lecturer in Early Years Education and programme leader for the Early Years Initial Teacher Training suite course at Nottingham Trent University. She has also delivered teaching on the childhood studies course, Masters in early years and BA (Hons) Education. She has a special interest in developing and sustaining quality childcare and learning experiences for young children.

Annie Woods has recently retired from Nottingham Trent University where she held a number of roles as an early years lecturer, programme leader and academic team leader. She developed a number of programmes and routes to early years qualifications and has been an external examiner in three universities. Prior to working in higher education, Annie taught in foundation stage and has been an assistant head teacher. She has edited three books: *Child-Initiated Play and Learning, The Characteristics of Effective Learning* and *Examining Levels of Involvement in the Early Years*, all for Routledge. Her own book, *Elemental Play and Outdoor Learning*, has recently been published.

Introduction

Annie Woods

Our aim with this book is to embrace emerging possibilities in children's play. Since writing the first edition, the authors have developed the possibilities theme in two further books, *The Characteristics of Effective Learning: Creating and capturing the possibilities in the early years* (2015) and *Examining Levels of Involvement in the Early Years: Engaging with children's possibilities* (2016). There are connections within the three books that have given us and the publisher the confidence to re-present our ideas which students and practitioners have reported as being useful and illuminative. Our subsequent research and reading have enabled us to enhance many of the chapters with further encounters and insights, while maintaining the essence of our established ideology and practice with students and practitioners who work in a very wide range of early years settings. There does seem to be a timelessness about this, in contrast to constantly changing guidance, policy, rhetoric and regulations and we ask readers to continue to be encouraged, provoked and challenged to re-think, re-search, re-visit, re-create and reflect. This book is free from any curriculum constraint, with learning at the heart of any teaching we consider. Readers can surmise, therefore, that *planning* and all that we understand of the organized preparation for future learning and teaching, should be guided by children's interests, and all those play and possibilities we have observed and delighted in. In Giugni's words, it remains timely to grant ourselves permission to question 'the way we have always done things' (cited in MacNaughton, 2005: 116), in the same way that very young children persist in asking 'why'.

The authors have a special interest in the early years and have worked alongside experienced practitioners, post and undergraduate students, and trainee teachers, who, as MacNaughton suggests, having joined the early years workforce 'are increasingly expected to concentrate on universal, predetermined outcomes and methods for achieving these outcomes, pressing the right button, crowding out possibilities to think, question, understand, discuss, contest and reflect' (2005: 11).

The current focus in England is on a paper-based planning trail, with an emphasis on a pre-determined journey towards a goal that can be tracked, measured and accomplished and we have often seen a curriculum cycle of long and medium term planning that narrowly represents a focus on learning areas, half terms or 'privileged' topics. They are privileged from adults' perspectives, and as tutors, we have attempted to challenge this established discourse with students and rather *foreground* MacNaughton's more engaging activities and emerging children's interests. We persist in embracing emerging possibilities, enabling you to grow in confidence in using presented opportunities, illustrative encounters and to enter a discursive space. We offer provocations to give room to the 'what takes place in-between' in what we see, what we interpret and what we do. With confidence, we argue you may be more ready, willing and able to engage with advisors, inspectors and leaders when presenting the evidence children have given you in the natural context of their play. This evidence will provide "more observational studies of children [. . .] undertaking playful tasks which are developmentally appropriate" and from which we may deduce children's "executive functioning and self-regulation". (Whitebread and Basilio, 2012). Curtis and O'Hagan have suggested that

> Bruce (1991) developed a view of play derived from the principle of Gleik's (1988) Chaos Theory. This theory is based on the view that the relationship between the process and the product in all systems is non-linear [thus messy, never finished and where new meanings shoot forth]. In play situations the observer is never entirely sure how the child is involved and what the child is getting out of it. As a result there is chaos and controversy inherent in the adults' interpretation of play and its value.
>
> (2003: 112)

These ideas resonate with the pedagogical approach adopted by Reggio pedagogues and educators in New Zealand and Sweden where the children are viewed as protagonists (they are able and want to start things); attuned adults are catalysts (the spark) and the environmental context full of possible and reflective journeys, a 'site for democratic and ethical practice' (Moss and Petrie, 2002: 2).

It seems more crucial than ever to consider diverse, cultural approaches and global pedagogies to enhance the experiences of our very youngest children. It is also heartening to note the recent 'pause' in the piloting of baseline assessment, which we suggest may reflect many settings' use of an assessment model based on natural observations, children's dispositions, levels of well-being and involvement and children's interests rather than more formulaic and narrow audits of specific outcomes. Chapter 7 is a thorough rationale for what may have occurred during 2015–16.

In this second edition, we remain committed to the child 'as an active and creative actor, as a subject and citizen with potentials . . .' (Dahlberg, 1997: 22, cited in Moss and Petrie, 2002) and aim to continue to create 'a crisis in people's thinking . . . opening up new possibilities and expectations, alternative enquiries and solutions, opportunities for new understandings and new ways of seeing . . .' (Moss and Petrie, 2002: 185). A crisis, a risk, an awkwardness can be scary, but it can also be marvelous and dynamic because faced with a puzzle or a paradox, we *have to do something*, and like children accommodating new information, adults need to remember and enjoy how to 'negotiate our different understandings, and learn about the diversities and differences in meaning-making and strategies of doing things' (Taguchi, 2010: 34). Consistent themes reflect a socio-constructive perspective, the idea that learning takes place mainly through the interaction with others, and the themes are influenced by esteemed international approaches to working with young children. The child is seen as a leader, learning independently, with peers and/or alongside attuned adults within reciprocal and valued relationships. The possibilities envisaged represent the child as fully participatory, a child with voice, autonomy and competence, learning within environments that *afford* an infinite number of possibilities. The environments may be emotional, social and physical, representing the emergence of the child into wider and wider communities. Our model for this closely follows Bronfenbrenner's Ecological Systems model where experienced environments resemble Russian dolls, with the child being the nested and nurtured centre, surrounded by and interacting with ever widening contexts. As practitioners, we can both support and enable the child and family, family and community, community and wider society to positively and dynamically interact. We also recognise that national and global contexts (political environments) will have an impact on our services and support for community, family and child.

The pedagogical ethos is one of playfulness, for *all children and adults*; we may define playful as actively engaging with unique ways of feeling, thinking and doing, whether this is transporting water in a teapot to the sand tray or creating and sharing a new administrative routine.

The authors, borrowing diverse ideas and approaches from varied disciplines, theories and research, illustrate their perspectives with a number of encounters in practice; again, the resonance with Reggio Emilia will be recognised. The encounters are authentic; they are not 'constructed' case studies but events, recollections and reflections that we have conceived with a view to establishing greater understanding of the ideas being discussed in each chapter. If you like, they are and have been part of our own learning journeys, illuminating elements of practice that have 'interrupted' our thinking. You may want to use these to start discussion and nourish shared encounters in your own setting.

We end each chapter with a series of provocations. Our intention is to be *awkward*, but not to take a critical stance. Having completed a sabbatical post as Assistant Head Teacher, a most effective staff development opportunity arose when I used similar provocative questions based on a reflective journal regarding encounters, conversations, observations and the rhetoric of policies as opposed to the practice sometimes experienced. Each encounter and provocation affords you a possibility; engaging with possibilities is, for us, a dynamic and meaningful part of planning, because having engaged with planning for possibilities you will be ready, willing and more able to 'go with the flow' and contest 'the way we have always done things'.

What you can do with the provocations is reflect upon them as an 'individual or collective'; you could take an encounter from Chapter 4 as an example. As described, most children are fascinated by insects and small animals. You can create naturally occurring possibilities for any child to find ladybirds in an exploratory rich environment; it is not necessary to plan an annual mini beast topic every May for all the children in your setting. The planning is in your research, the anticipation of, and having the resources ready, to follow the children's interests and the willingness to interpret and assess this shared learning as it happens.

There have been many, many times when, having anticipated the direction a child might take with an interest or schema, I have collected resources and considered potential and extending activities and carried out some research of my own on, say, the ladybird life cycle. I then find the child's own enquiries have gone in a completely different direction. This is to be celebrated . . . and expected! The reflection and 'preparedness' has occurred; it is not wasted. It is ready for another child's direction and you are *more prepared*.

Each chapter offers ideas to be considered. In Chapter 1, Catherine argues that planning the learning environment is *how* practitioners can plan for endless possibilities. The physical learning environment, resources, emotional milieu, children's interests and organisation are considered as aspects of the learning environment. It is argued that children need extended periods of time to play, to follow their interests, and to be valued as competent learners; they also thrive in secure relationships and are more able to explore significant questions and access open-ended resources. The idea of determinable ability is challenged as a limiting factor and practitioners' belief in endless possibilities is deemed to be crucial as they support, enable and model limitless learning.

Vicky introduces the notion of parental involvement, in Chapter 2, as a key aspect of all early years curricula, policy and practice and while many practitioners believe that they have good relationships with parents, this relationship is often at an operational level rather than a truly reciprocal and balanced one. A balanced, reciprocal relationship involves parents fully in planning for their children's holistic development and learning. This chapter offers a range of encounters that explore the many dimensions of this complex aspect of early years work across the age range. Drawing on a wide range of perspectives and approaches such as Reggio Emilia and Te Whāriki it offers many strategies for working with parents, including home visiting, opportunities for parents to play and learn alongside their children and sharing documentation. These strategies work towards empowering parents to become more fully involved in their children's learning, thus creating for them a role in their children's life in the setting and supporting the at-home learning environment. This chapter offers provocations that the reader can reflect on both as an individual practitioner and as a staff team, considering how they can develop and strengthen their relationships with parents.

Moira, in Chapter 3, 'Exploring the possibilities of children's voice', considers issues of voice, advocacy and participation for those working with the youngest children. Taking the United Nation Convention on the Rights of the Child (UNCRC) (1989) as the catalyst for development in the field of a rights-based pedagogy, the chapter tracks key developments in the field. Within this contextual background, the role of the practitioner is presented and challenges discussed. A socio-constructive perspective presents children as powerful social agents from birth, and indicates possibilities for listening to, hearing and involving the youngest children in a community of participation. Witnessed examples illustrate everyday potential in practice for the perceptive and receptive practitioner. The chapter ends with a review of the wide benefits of a listening pedagogy, both immediate and long-term, validating the approach beyond the meeting of requirements.

In 'Exploiting outdoor possibilities for all children', Chapter 4, Annie and Val demonstrate the increasing awareness of the opportunities for planning and provision when considering inclusive outdoor play. Through a series of encounters, to possible challenges and barriers, some real and some self-imposed, we guide adults on a journey to develop their confidence and commitment. The promotion of inclusive practice supported through legislation and the understanding of the benefits of the outdoors provides a realistic perspective on this occasionally perplexing environment. Thought-provoking conversations help to address nervousness and inexperience and suggest that through training, support and allegiance with more-confident peers, fears and concerns may be successfully addressed and overcome. The nature of inclusive friendly spaces considers the interplay of factors ranging from architectural structures, diverse environments and natural experiences, to personal constructs impacting on our pedagogy of play in the outdoors. The advantage of inclusive outdoor play is linked to a willingness and desire to promote it.

Chapter 5 is about encouraging adults working with young children to allow them to engage more in adventurous play scenarios than they do at present. It aims to promote confidence in adults to plan for opportunities to develop encounters in children's play, recognising the huge benefits to children's development when they have to consider and manage risks themselves. It focuses particularly on adults' reassessment of risk, adventure and challenge, and the physical environment and materials that will promote adventurous play. Finally, the chapter wishes to provoke adults' beliefs about children's risk competencies by providing evidence that children are able to manage risks themselves if potential hazards are reduced. She encourages us to really consider our approaches to risk and play.

With an insightful approach, Victoria and Moira consider 'Play as a space for possibilities' in Chapter 6 and explore the position of play in settings, and how it can be foregrounded in planning to protect its special place for children in indoor and outdoor experiences. Acknowledgement is given to some of the influences that may currently challenge play provision, and a positive perspective on play suggested in response. A socio-constructive stance perceives the child as powerful in play, constructing meanings, creating ideas and expressing agency. This construct of play as one of the child's many voices indicates possible responses from the practitioner within a valuing and enabling pedagogy. Encounters in practice illustrate the argument, evidencing that '*all play* is purposeful and meaningful *to the player*', and proposing appropriate, opportune and timely interventions in a partnership of co-construction.

Victoria continues this idea in Chapter 7, 'The possibilities for assessment'; conceptualising assessment as a continuous process of seeking to know and understand children and their unique and individual approaches to learning, this chapter considers a range of holistic and observational approaches to assessment drawn from international and national practice. Influenced by theories of social constructivism and the image of children as capable and confident learners who can play an active part in the assessment process, the role of feedback and sustained shared thinking is explored. Recognising that assessment cannot be separated from the social, emotional and cultural context within which it occurs, this chapter also considers the importance of assessing children's wellbeing and documenting the interactions of groups of children engaged in meaningful contexts for learning. While acknowledging the challenges of assessment in practice, practitioners are urged to reflect on the purposes of their assessment in order to fully appreciate what the process of assessment can add to their developing understanding of children and families and to their own practice and procedures as a setting. In this way practitioners will be able to take an informed approach to assessment, adopting the approaches that will work best in the richness of their own contexts and that they truly value and taking steps to challenge those practices that are deemed unworkable.

Chapter 8, 'Leading possibilities', presents a dialogue between two colleagues, Annie and Lorna, who consider the questions, challenges and dilemmas faced by lead practitioners across a range of early years settings. The majority of questions have been raised during visits to, and while supporting, leaders and managers who represent the complexity of roles and contexts within early years. A dialogic stance has been taken to model an approach of working together, and reflects the training, mentoring, advising and working alongside staff and students undertaken over many years. As in other chapters, the aim is to co-construct understanding based on shared reflections and recognise the interplay between dynamic and emerging cultural contexts: community interests, economic and demographic change, the balance between the needs of the individual child/setting/local and national strategic goals and the interpersonal relationships between new, current and well established employees. Authentic encounters present useful starting points of discussion for teams and a staff development opportunity and it is anticipated that these conversations will open up many further possibilities for adults 'to affirm, to welcome, to challenge, to question, to try out, be critical, be uncertain, to listen and negotiate'; for leaders to begin to transform their practice.

References

Curtis, A. and O'Hagan, M. (2003) *Care and Education in Early Childhood: A Student's Guide to Theory and Practice*. London: RoutledgeFalmer

MacNaughton, G. (2005) *Doing Foucault in Early Childhood Studies: Applying poststructural ideas*. London: Routledge

Moss, P. and Petrie, P. (2002) *From Children's Services to Children's Spaces: Public policy, children and childhood*. London: RoutledgeFalmer

Taguchi, H. L. (2010) *Going beyond the Theory/Practice Divide in Early Childhood Education: Introducing an intra-active pedagogy*. London: Routledge

Whitehead, D. and Basilio, M. (2012) *The emergence and early development of self-regulation in young children*. Profesorado. Revista de curriculum y formacion del profesorado. Vol. 16. No 1 (enero–abril 2012). www.ugr.es/recfpro/rev161ART2en.pdf (accessed 6/6/16)

Woods, A. Ed. (2015) *The Characteristics of Effective Learning: Creating and capturing the possibilities in the early years*. London: David Fulton.

Woods, A. Ed. (2016) *Examining Levels of Involvement in the Early Years: Engaging with children's possibilities*. London: David Fulton

1

Planning for endless possibilities

Catherine Gripton

Planning can often be considered an adult activity, where practitioners decide what should be learned, when and how, almost seeing into the future for how the learning experience will be. Planning is translated into practice, which is then evaluated according to whether children have met the learning goals set. Within this model of teaching and learning, control and responsibility lie firmly with the practitioner, their knowledge of each child and skill in designing activities. Here practitioners carry a heavy burden as directors and deliverers of learning. They can experience the guilt of not having sufficient knowledge of each child they work with (sometimes for only a few hours a week) and feel unable to differentiate planning for every child's needs. They can also feel the guilt of not having spent 'enough' time with each child to help them realise the learning that was formed in the practitioner's head when planning. Regardless of the effort, skill and knowledge of the practitioner, learning is limited, the child can be passive and the practitioner exhausted. There is another way. Planning for possibilities rather than outcomes switches the dynamics of planning. Here, the practitioner's role is to facilitate learning (to follow rather than to lead). The control and responsibility is more balanced in its distribution, thus resting much more with the child. The plans are determined by an 'insider', the child, supported and enabled by the practitioner.

This book establishes a clear rationale for planning for possibilities and the rewards that it brings for practitioners, parents and all children in terms of learning and well-being. It examines removing limits on learning through being rooted in real-world, hands-on, experiential learning; planning and preparing for the possible paths, directions, interests and activities that could arise without narrowing, or indeed forcing, these possibilities. This chapter specifically considers how we can plan for further possibilities leading to endless possibilities: for the unknown as well as the known, for the possibilities which we cannot or do not foresee and to become 'comfortable with the unknown' (Malaguzzi, 1994: 3). It may seem illogical to suggest that we can 'plan' for endless possibilities but our planning can support children in following endless possibilities and moreover can, through continuous provision (available to the children all the time), provide a context that contains the potential for inclusive and unlimited learning.

The learning environment is the conduit of learning for the child, where planning the *context* for learning is *how* we plan for endless possibilities. Planning is complex and multi-faceted as it includes all the constituent aspects and contributory factors that fluidly combine to create the learning environment. In planning each aspects such as the physical learning environment (one entity, indoors and outdoors), resources, emotional milieu and organisation, we have to consider the interplay between each of these in addition to each individual aspect. Thus endless possibilities can be planned for through varied and carefully structured 'safe' spaces; areas of activity; accessible open-ended resources; the facilitation of secure relationships; following children's interests and extended periods of free-play. Practitioners have a crucial role within this, not just as planners of provision but also as believers in the infinite possibilities it encompasses and in enabling and encouraging children to explore them. The impact of the early learning environment upon children's learning is life-long and cumulative (Fisher, 2008); it is enabling, inclusive and limitless and is therefore crucial in order for it to provide for aspirational endless possibilities in the child's present and future learning. Whitebread and Basilio (2012: 16) refer to Vygotsky (1978) when they clearly argue, these 'higher mental processes [are] involved in self-regulation', 'currently attracting considerable and rapidly growing attention'.

The physical learning environment: the context for endless possibilities

> The environment is the mechanism by which the early childhood educator brings the child and the different aspects of knowledge together.
>
> (Bruce, 2011: 66)

The physical learning environment is crucially important in mediating between learning and the child, anchoring and connecting them, almost as an interpreter between the two. As is suggested, different areas and aspects of learning are integrated together within a concrete experience or activity. As each experience exists with and within many experiences (Boud, Cohen and Walker, 1993), this is an increasingly complex picture. Where curricula are arranged into subject areas or disciplines, it might also seem sensible to organise the physical learning environment into these same areas. This can be perceived as addressing curriculum 'coverage', balance and access issues and as simplifying assessment and staffing structures. Such a decision is premised on the assumption that children's learning can be similarly compartmentalised and that certain activities or resources always lead to particular types of learning, that learning is essentially homogenous, unconnected and ultimately limited. If learning was this simple and orderly it would lead to problems when applying it to real world experiences, such as parking a car or planning a day trip, which do not come with labels for which area of learning is needed or indeed the time to use each individually. Conversely, learning is actually complex and holistic, enabling us to make many varied, interrelated connections simultaneously and to think creatively. It is vital in planning for endless possibilities that the physical learning environment is attuned authentically to the nature of learning and the unique nature of childhood.

Children naturally blend and apply a range of understanding to each activity they engage with, for example using scientific observation, artistic expression, mathematical spatial awareness and physical fine motor skills (among others) to create a painting. To plan for endless possibilities, therefore, we should organise the physical learning environment into areas of activity, where all types of learning can be developed in each space, hereby conceptualising them as physical spaces for *activity or resources* rather than areas for *learning*. Adhering to this principle can be challenging when practitioners feel pressure (from managers, leaders, parents

---

ENCOUNTER: Observing the 'maths table'

In my capacity as mathematics coordinator, I visited the school nursery one morning to do a planned observation of maths teaching and learning. I was ushered to a seat next to the maths table, which was a table with shelves of labelled baskets containing calculators, threading beads, cubes, sorting trays, brightly coloured small animals, number lines, compare bears, plastic shapes and rulers. The children were busy around the indoor and outdoor nursery environment; few children approached the maths table. Occasionally a child would collect a small animal and make an animal noise or pick up a calculator and use it as a walkie-talkie or press buttons idly while looking around the room before returning it to its basket and moving on to another activity. One of the practitioners offered individual or groups of children encouragement to use the table and its resources but there were no takers. After twenty minutes, I had seen no mathematical learning.

Whether the area was named a mathematical learning area or not appeared to have no bearing upon whether mathematical learning occurred there. At the end of the observation time, I discussed my observations with the lead practitioners who explained the frustration they felt that children did not choose to do mathematical activities and asked how they could 'liven up' the maths table. For me, the issue was not the maths table (although I advised them to dispense of it in favour of a pattern area or puzzle table) but the compartmentalisation of learning into subject areas and then physical areas of the environment. There was an enormous amount of child-initiated mathematical activity occurring that morning across the nursery when playing with books, sand, dough, water, bikes, mark-making materials, blocks, jigsaws, etc. This learning could have been developed, extended and multiplied many times over if practitioners had planned, recognised and supported rich mathematical opportunities across all physical areas in the continuous provision. Conversely, the drive for 'curriculum coverage' and providing opportunities for all areas of learning had led the practitioners down a path that limited the possibilities for learning and experience.

or inspectors) to improve children's experiences and achievement in individual subjects or areas of learning, particularly if practitioners feel that these will be scrutinised singly. Working within these pressures, scope still exists to plan for areas of activity rather than learning. This can be as simple as the names given to spaces or areas within the physical learning environment, where subtle differences convey clear messages to children and parents about the nature of learning. It also infers that technology can be present in any area; children should and can be encouraged to both record their interests, building, pattern making and artefacts as well as access and scrutinise further information about the materials they are using and activities associated with that area. A 'book corner' is where books are stored, can be taken and returned to wherein a broad range of learning can occur. This is different from a 'reading corner', which is for reading and learning to read, suggesting that reading occurs only with books and only in one specific place across all of the continuous provision (perhaps excluding places outside of the educational setting). To plan for endless possibilities is to plan for them in every part of the physical learning environment. Here the planning involves carrying out research yourself into any additional resources that a child can use to extend or integrate diverse materials into their activity. I recall a child returning from a holiday where they had climbed inside a windmill and become interested in trying to make one. We used online resources to find many images and diagrams of working windmills, including the one visited, storing images and printing some out to display in the building in the mathematics, making and reading areas.

Within the physical learning environment the indoor and outdoor are one provider, which consists of a range of spaces that include places where the children have the opportunity to be together and alone, with or without a practitioner (Gandini, 1993). Where these are comfortable, safe and stimulating places that can be revisited many times (providing familiar or new experiences), they foster endless possibilities for communication, engagement, imagination and meaningful development. As the 'maths table' encounter suggests, children are not attracted and engaged by subjects so much as resources and contexts. It is therefore important for these to feel accessible and inviting and form a range of diverse spaces across the continuous provision. Variety across the indoor and outdoor environments is key, as both spaces offer distinctly different experiences and, as explored in Chapter 4, should not replicate each other. Each space in the physical learning environment should be open-ended and distinctive while remaining authentic within its context. Authentic contexts recognise the potential and possibilities that exist naturally; they support meaningful activity and enable learning to organically develop. Whitebread and Basilio (2012: 20) refer to earlier research by Whitebread (2005, 2007, 2009) who carried out

> observational studies of children in naturalistic contexts of their pre-school classrooms, mostly engaging in playful, self-initiated individual and small group collaborative activities. In this type of context, these observations have revealed extensive self-regulatory behaviours in this age group, including examples of both the complimentary processes of monitoring and control. Monitoring

behaviours observed in preschool children included self-commentary, reviewing progress and keeping track, rating effort and level of difficulty, checking behaviours and detecting errors, evaluating strategies used, rating the quality of performance, and evaluating when a task was complete. Control behaviours included changing strategies as a result of previous monitoring, applying a previously learnt strategy to a new situation, repeating a strategy in order to check the accuracy of the outcome, using a non-verbal gesture to support cognitive activity, and various types of planning activity.

In very young children, however, these abilities are very context dependent. The context relies upon the skilful and possibility planning of practitioners to afford the opportunity to self-regulate.

Resources: representing endless possibilities

> Anything the child makes or does can be seen as an expression of their understanding of the world around them. Their inner thoughts are demonstrated in the outer representations they make in which-ever media they choose.
>
> (Whinnett, 2012: 128)

Children need the resources and tools with which they can represent their ideas, understanding and feelings, their interpretation of themselves and their world (Bruner, 1990). There are endless possibilities as to the shape and form of their understanding and how they would like to represent this, different for each unique individual and continually changing and evolving. Endless resources are not practical; therefore the resources that are the daily diet of children within the continuous provision need to be sufficiently open-ended to contain the potential to become an infinite range of representations. Resources that have limited uses and possibilities will in turn limit and narrow children's thinking, excluding many children who think and act in lateral ways. Some resources are designed to lead to only one use, limiting the possibilities for symbolic representation, requiring the child to see beyond the adults' intended use – to imagine in spite of the resource. In planning for endless possibilities, *we do not ask what it is but what it could be and what it can be used for.*

In early years settings, resource acquisition can be haphazard with many resources inherited, donated or purchased intermittently and by different managers. The encounter with Thomas refers to the 'coveting' of resources where some resources in a setting can become high status, much sought-after items (exacerbated by feelings of insecurity). For individual children, to have the item is the initial priority, then comes keeping it, inevitably what follows is regaining the resource when it is lost to another and so it continues. In this situation the practitioner's worthy efforts to promote fairness and sharing can do little to prevent the preoccupation of possession and only serve to regulate or adapt the cycle. Learning is secondary to possession and children often do little with the resource once they

ENCOUNTER: Thomas and the capes

Across the setting, there were one or two popular outfits that were the first ones chosen each session, with some children choosing the same outfit almost every day. There were approximately ten outfits in the area, with most commonly up to four being used at any one time. When worn by the children, some played in character but more often they used props for this (real and imagined) and children wore the clothes while playing something unrelated to the outfit. When asked, the children said they were the person you might guess from their attire, often a pirate, doctor or princess, but did not seem to be playing in role. I wanted the clothes to be less limiting and more open-ended and to do more to encourage imaginative role-play but was concerned to remove resources that seemed popular, particularly with children such as Thomas.

Thomas (a 3-year-old) would select a yellow and orange fireman's tabard almost every session but never stayed in the role-play area; he would then go to play with the train, blocks or water. Through observing Thomas it appeared that he was not 'in role' but rather liked the comfort and security of wearing the tabard. If this item was not available he would take a different jacket and put that on instead. I wondered if he used the tabard as a way of making first contact with an adult in the setting, as he would take it to them to help him put it on. It seemed to be part of his routine, a way of transitioning from home to nursery.

With this in mind, we felt able to make the change (with the tabard nearby just in case). The clothes that led themselves to only one role or character were removed and replaced by six different coloured capes in each area, which could also be worn over clothes as skirts. The capes became many different characters, some known but many invented. The role-play area became more popular and was accessed by a greater range of children. The resources did not mitigate against children changing and adapting their characters while they played and there was less 'coveting' of particular favourite items. A Superman cape can only be a Superman cape. A plain red cape can be Little Red Riding Hood, Superman, a Postal worker or a new or invented character and with several capes you could have more than one superman. The children could become the character in the book that we had just read with the resource to make this feel safe. The possibility to be any character had always existed but the support to enable children to see and believe these possibilities had not.

have it except try to protect their ownership rights. The origin of the enhanced status of a specific resource can be difficult to pinpoint and sometimes passed on between generations of children attending the setting. In planning for endless possibilities we select and present resources in the most flexible and open-ended way possible, avoiding having too many very different or distinctive versions of the same thing. Sometimes, it may be better to have several of the same cape or several plain capes than a jumble of different outfits that are limiting and can become status bearing.

In seeking out the most rich, open-ended resources that contain the potential for endless possibilities, nature is our greatest provider. Natural resources are varied, unique, sensory, stimulating, interesting and flexible. They sit comfortably with and complement other resources and raise infinite questions and lines of enquiry. In planning outdoor continuous provision, there are practical limits to including larger natural areas and resources, such as trees, ponds and rocks. We can, however, embrace the readily available remembering that, 'the outdoors is at your fingertips, be it a balcony, a back-yard, a porch, or a playground. It is a place just waiting to be explored' (Ward, 2008: 18). For use indoors and outdoors, collections of natural objects and materials (such as pieces of driftwood, bark, pebbles, stones, leaves, conkers, pine cones, shells, sticks, sand, mud; see Chapter 4) provide open-ended resources, rich in variety, textures and opportunities to explore, which can be regularly replenished.

While there are challenges for practitioners in creating our own resources, as these can be carefully planned, we can ensure that they are rich in potential possibilities. Brock *et al.* (2009) argue that through creating resources, practitioners are creative themselves and more fully consider how they can scaffold children's learning, thinking critically about purpose and potential. Through the designing and making process practitioners begin to see the possibilities that the resource might hold for the different children they work with. Creating resources as a team can therefore also be a fruitful basis for focussed professional dialogue about possibilities.

Children's interests: following the endless possibilities

> There will be times when children are particularly fascinated by and interested in particular things. They need the time and personal space and help to focus on their interests, from which they will learn deeply, provided everything in the learning environment indoors and outdoors is carefully thought through and presented with educational possibilities.
>
> (Bruce, 2012: 159)

Children's interests are catalysts of endless possibilities. In planning for this, we are valuing children as competent learners. In planning to follow children's interests, it is important to conceptualise the notion within its broadest terms – to consider what children find interesting. The enormous breadth of children's interests, we contest, may not fully be reflected in what society, consumers and some families deem as most important. It is also important to be cautious of following children's interests as a device purely to motivate learning, to help adults achieve their goals for the child rather than to take a child-led journey together. Woods (2016b) considers this in more detail, highlighting a sociocultural transitional perspective, mediated learning, guided participation, joint attention and sustained shared thinking as crucial to this reciprocal journey. Children's interests commonly overlap and are developed and explored together as shared interests, often related to broader human interests.

ENCOUNTER: The jumper

We were able to take frequent walks into the nearby woodland, to record with our senses, the smells, sounds and touch of changing seasons. One of our children with ASD was reluctant to leave the classroom but after being given the camera to look through and take photographs if he wished, he joined the end of our walking line, just behind his keyworker who was very sensitive to both his needs and presence. When we returned to the classroom, Liam loaded his photographs onto the computer and we used them in recall time to share our experience. All of the photographs were of the cable pattern on his keyworker's jumper. He was unable to explain what the fascination was, but they were exquisite close-ups and he showed great pleasure in looking at them on a large screen. We discussed this as a staff team and our planning took a new turn. The following day, we asked Liam to choose his favourites, and he helped us to print them onto A3, feed them into the laminator, then place them in the painting and making areas. They proved to be very provocative both in discussions about Marie's jumper and what the pattern was called, who else had jumpers like hers, but also in the patterns and textures we provided and were experienced for the next few weeks. Liam was highly valued for this new plan and the resulting attention from his peers who would show him their paintings, rubbings and models. We began to resource a textured knitting box and some large knitting needles should the interest

Considering each child within their own environmental, social and cultural context (Bronfenbrenner, 1979) helps us to understand that children's interests are located within the boundaries of their experiences. It is therefore vital to broaden their experiences and present them with a wide range of opportunities to take an interest within their context. Families, as part of the child's context, know much about children's interests and how these have developed for each child. Practitioners have an important role in establishing open and on–going dialogue within which a picture and shared understanding of the child's interests can emerge while also helping to bridge what Athey (2007: 201) referred to as the 'gulf' between parents and professionals. Practitioner observation and communication are essential in illuminating and informing the emerging picture of a child's interests while being mindful not to distort what we learn, as it is filtered through adult layers of interpretation. For example, we might interpret an interest to be in 'lorries and tractors' where the interest is more about rotation and turning.

In the encounter, Klaudia needs to capture and represent what she observes, to recreate in order to explore more fully. She might do this through paint, pastel, writing, drawing, clay, collage, video, water play, talk, experimentation, dance or movement (or several of these over time). It is important (and sometimes challenging) to give Klaudia the time and space and freedom to follow her interest but this alone is insufficient. She needs the tools and experiences to enable her to do so. When the wild horses of possibilities are about to run free, she needs the

---

ENCOUNTER: Klaudia's puddle

Over a fifteen-minute period, I noticed Klaudia looking out of the window in the classroom. Each time I looked over, she was looking at a fixed point on the ground outside. She had opened the window as wide as possible and was looking through the gap, the open window sheltering her head from the heavy rain. Several children had joined her for a few minutes looking at the same spot and then moved on but Klaudia remained there, seemingly unaware of the many activities going on in the classroom behind her. I went over to Klaudia and joined her leaning out of the window as best I could. Following her gaze, I could see that she was looking at a small puddle on the path that had rain drops falling in it. After a few moments she noticed I was next to her and turned, hesitated then smiled at me before returning her attention to the puddle. 'I'm watching the shapes in the puddle' she said, 'I'm working out when they will touch, can *you* see?'

As the drops of rain splashed into the puddle, Klaudia was apparently predicting where and when the circular ripples would meet, perhaps looking for winners and losers or changes to the patterns. Noticing is important in learning. In noticing we find what is the same or different, spot changes over time, see patterns or anomalies, adjusting our understanding according to this new piece of data. These skills are developed in many fields of study including Maths, Science, History and Geography and used in many real-life situations. Noticing a puddle and observing changes in the shapes holds many possibilities for learning important skills and concepts. However, as a busy practitioner with many pressures, these can be missed. She might have been 'told off' for not doing the activity that had been 'planned' by the adult, her actions considered to be 'daydreaming' or 'wasting time'.

---

saddle, step and horse–riding experience to be able to ride one to see where it will take her. Without the appropriate tools and relevant experiences, potential avenues of learning will remain unexplored.

Following careful examination of what is important and interesting to our children, to support children in following a possible pathway in learning, we can encourage them to formulate 'questions worth asking' (Rich *et al.*, 2006). Challenging and interesting, these big questions promote creative thinking, encourage connection-making and involve issues of generality and conceptual understanding. In order to create an environment in which big questions are asked we must avoid small questions. Questions such as 'what is this book called? or 'what did we do yesterday?' are disingenuous as teachers already know the answers so children realise that the questions are artificial (Fisher, 2008). The absurdity of these types of questions is that they can often be answered even when listening at the most superficial of levels or by guessing what the questioner is thinking about. Artificial questions do not value children; they insult their intelligence, model poor speaking and listening skills, and encourage the children to be passive or dependent. Many are not actually questions at all, more instructions or behaviour management strategies packaged as a question. To support children in finding and following their interests we need to help them develop their ability to ask big questions through experiencing them. As practitioners we need to ask children questions to which we ourselves are uncertain of the answer or to which many answers exist; we can ask questions without expecting a definitive answer or sometimes an answer at all. Exploring these questions will take hours, days or weeks rather than seconds and may need to be communicated in many different ways. Children can be agents of endless possibilities, where we do more than create an environment in which children *can* ask big questions but where children *do* ask big questions.

Organisation: enabling the endless possibilities

Organisation is an aspect of practitioner planning that can scaffold endless possibilities through providing time, consistency and continuity that supports children and practitioners in exploring possibilities. Uninterrupted chunks of free-flow time for children to play and extended periods of time for practitioners to play with children can be difficult to achieve in busy settings but significant in enabling possibilities to become realities. Breaks within these periods of free-flow play are often necessary (for meals, group times and ends of session) but for a child they can come at the mid-point of an activity in which they are immersed. Shared group times are an important feature of early years practice and also open up possibilities for children through experiences that provide access to children's literature or group singing for example. While we cannot and should not avoid these breaks, we can endeavour to value children's activity through how they are managed. This can include limiting the number of breaks and ensuring that these are at regular times each day, preparing children to leave their activity and ensuring that activities can be returned to (perhaps by using 'work in progress' or name signs). It is also important to recognise that for some children the number of breaks or interruptions can be significantly higher than others, even within the same setting. Special interest, support or intervention groups can add to a more stuttered timetable for some children. Children who attend a setting for fewer hours might also find less time to follow and explore their own ideas and interests where they are expected to have participated in the same number of adult-led activities as other children who attend the setting for more hours.

Organisational features of settings impact upon how much children follow possibilities, whether they feel that this is important to the people around them and how far they believe that endless possibilities exist within their own learning. Children need to feel secure in their relationships therefore the organisation of the setting needs to provide consistency in these relationships as well as time for these to develop. Self-esteem can be negatively affected by organisational structures where they communicate messages to children and families about achievement and developmental expectations and damage perceptions of the child as a competent and successful learner. Such organisational structures include grouping systems, the presentation of documentation of learning and delegation of staff responsibilities, which all impact upon the emotional learning environment and are therefore a key consideration.

Emotional milieu: feeling the endless possibilities

In planning for endless possibilities we need to remove barriers to what is possible or more importantly to what children, parents and practitioners *believe* is possible. It may seem obvious to state that we need to perceive each child as a competent learner, however to truly achieve this we need to demonstrate that we value all the things that the child can do and likes to do, including the way and context in which they learn as in Liam's encounter with the jumper. To value the child is to value what they like to do, their interests and the people and activities that are important to them. These are the foundations of an emotional learning environment in which endless possibilities exist. The social context for learning within the emotional milieu is supported by the continuity of provision in terms of the relationships with adults but also the relationships with peers in the setting; a particular issue for settings where children attend for different sessions, or have regular individual and small support group activities throughout the week. Photographs and video can be utilised well to support the feeling that children belong to the setting even when they are not there. Relationships cannot be planned for but planning can support and facilitate their development, sustaining them through regular time together allowing them to change and evolve.

The children's perception of what we, as practitioners, value is an important contributor to the emotional learning environment. We communicate this through which activities we praise and reward and where we place ourselves physically within the setting throughout each session. This communicates much to parents, colleagues and children about what we value and feel is important in learning. Where balance does not exist, albeit unintentionally, a two-tier system can become established where learning activities are deemed as either more or less important. When children are taken away while immersed in their own choice activity to engage in an adult-led activity, the child is given a clear message that the adult-led activity is more important for learning. This is confounded when the activity is high status, or for something 'important' from the child's perspective (e.g. for a performance, greetings card or display); it can also exclude many children who are unable or do not wish to participate. Where adult-led or specific areas of continuous provision feel more important, an environment is created in which children do not feel confident or empowered to follow their own ideas. Similarly, an emotional milieu supportive of endless possibilities has an atmosphere where risk-taking is commonplace, where it is deemed to be an essential aspect of learning and as such is actively promoted by practitioners. As explored in Chapter 5, the confidence to take risks in learning is dependent upon self-esteem alongside feelings of inclusion, belonging and security. Planning for endless possibilities should therefore seek to foster and promote such feelings throughout all aspects of the learning environment.

Planning for endless possibilities is not truly possible if we perceive ability to be fixed, finite or limited. This notion suggests that there are pre-determined limits for every child's learning (Swann et al., 2012) and that these limits can be greater for some children. Where we plan or expect less of certain children, the possibilities for these children are lessened. Hart et al. (2004) challenge the misconception that ability is a fixed point, explaining that this view is maintained in education as it offers what is thought to be an explanation for individual differences but is actually unhelpful and potentially damaging. Language such as 'high, medium or low ability', 'average' and 'levels' (including 'expected levels') describe limits to possible learning and are incompatible with planning for endless possibilities. In doing so, we accept that planning for a child as they currently are can inhibit their learning (and be a limiting factor in whom they may become). In short, we need to plan for the child's future potential rather than current attainment.

Practitioners are crucial in supporting children to follow their ideas, explore and discover; fundamentally to help children see the world of possibilities around them. As practitioners we need to embody the endless possibilities that we wish to provide for our children, if we believe that anything is possible then we increase the potential for these possibilities to become reality. As practitioners, this comes from our individual values and beliefs about children and the nature of learning. Where our view of the child is as a competent co-constructor of learning then the child is a 'powerful partner' (Soler and Miller, 2003). From this standpoint, we can create the conducive, supportive and inclusive environments that are 'hot houses' for endless possibilities.

Endless possibilities for the future

In planning for endless possibilities we value children and childhood. We provide time and space in possibility rich environments with practitioners who model, scaffold and embrace possibilities and thus we 'tool up' our children to explore what is possible. Instead of every child each working on their own project, the result is a fluid interplay of overlapping areas of human interest explored without limits, sometimes together, sometimes alone. As practitioners, we look at a group of children and see infinite possibilities, knowing that there are more that you cannot see and more that are yet to be formed. We can provide the context where some of these possibilities will begin to unfold with no way of knowing which ones will come, where and how. This is not to say that in planning for endless possibilities we are planning for random unknown outcomes, on the contrary, they will be born out of the patterns, interests and schemas of each individual child and will be contextualised within their immediate cultural influences (Athey, 2012), relationships and environment.

Preparing and enabling endless possibilities is as much about belief and faith as it is about practicalities. With the commitment to providing a learning environment that is conducive to endless possibilities, we take practical steps towards making them a reality and move from planning for limited outcomes to planning for inclusive, limitless learning. In perceiving the world as ever-changing moment to moment, we acknowledge endless possibilities and at the same time simplify our task as educators and pardon ourselves from the impossible task of pre-determining the future. In this we need to feel more confident in learning outcomes revealed naturally through self-regulatory play; then we can plan for the children's real futures accepting that we should not know what these will be.

Provocations

- Where do you spend time in your setting? Are you outdoors as much as indoors? Do you spend time on the floor, at tables, on mats and beanbags? Would the children be surprised if you climbed, rode a bike or lay on the floor?

- Do you show that you value an infinite range of activities through the praise you give children? Do you praise children's writing more than construction? Do you display paintings that look like something to you as well as ones that appear more abstract? Do you ask children to audit the value of your environment through a mosaic approach?

- Considering the children you work with, do they associate certain activities with particular members of staff? If all practitioners are seen to do all activities does this prevent them from modelling following their own interests?

- Do you and your colleagues agree about when and how to intervene in children's play? When is it okay to disrupt play: to have a snack, read to an adult, toilet reminders, join in a group activity? How can you make an effort to ensure that children's choices are valued when you do this? When time is tight, is it adult-led activity or children's choice activity that is sacrificed?

- Does every question we ask children need to have a definitive answer or be possible to answer in under a minute or an hour? Who should ask more questions, children or practitioners? What might the benefits be of children and adults asking 'big questions'?

- Due to the holistic nature of learning, this chapter argues for planning physical areas of activity rather than areas of learning. Are there any areas of learning or subject areas that you feel might be underrepresented if planning continuous provision in this way? What might cause this? How could this be addressed?

- Look at the resources that you have planned to use every day or are part of the provision which children have continuous access to. How many different possibilities or uses can you see in the first few seconds of looking at an area or resource in your setting? Are children allowed to mix resources across several areas? Do practitioners model this in their play?

- How 'in control' do you like to feel in terms of planning? Do you find it scary to prepare for times when the children will make the decisions and not you? How might you become a more 'risk-taking' practitioner in this regard?

- What are the main barriers to endless possibilities? How might you reduce these? Are attitudes a factor?

References

Athey, C. (2007) *Extending Thought in Young Children: A Parent-Teacher Partnership*, London: PCP.

Athey, C. (2012) Beginning with the theory about schemas. In: Arnold, C. (ed.) *Young Children Learning Through Schemas*, Oxford: Routledge.

Boud, D., Cohen, R. and Walker, D. (eds) (1993) *Using Experience for Learning*, Buckingham, UK: OUP.

Brock, A., Dodds, S., Jarvis, P. and Olusoga, Y. (2009) *Perspectives on Play: Learning for Life*, Essex, UK: Pearson.

Bronfenbrenner, U. (1979) *The Ecology of Human Development: Experiments by Nature and Design*, London: Harvard University Press.

Bruce, T. (2011) *Early Childhood Education*, 4th edn, London: Hodder.

Bruce, T. (ed.) (2012) *Early Childhood Practice: Froebel today*, London: Sage.

Bruner, J. S. (1990) *Acts of Meaning*, London: Harvard University Press.

Fisher, J. (2008) *Starting from the Child: Teaching and Learning in the Foundation Stage*, Berkshire, UK: OUP.

Gandini, L. (1993) Fundamentals of the Reggio Emilia approach to early childhood education, *Young Children*, 49(1): 4–8.

Hart, S., Dixon, A., Drummond, M. J. and McIntyre, D. (2004) *Learning without Limits*, Maidenhead, UK: Open University Press.

Malaguzzi, L. (1994) Your image of the child: where teaching begins. Available online at: www.reggioalliance.org/downloads/malaguzzi:ccie:1994.pdf (accessed 6 December 2011).

Rich, D., Casanova, D., Dixon, A., Drummond, M. J., Durrant, A. and Myer, C. (2006) *First Hand Experience: What Matters to Children*, Ipswich, UK: Rich Learning Opportunities.

Soler, J. and Miller, L. (2003) The struggle for early childhood curricula: a comparison of the English Foundation Stage Curriculum, Te Whāriki and Reggio Emilia, *International Journal of Early Years Education*, 11(1): 57–68.

Swann, M., Peacock, A., Hart, S. and Drummond, M. J. (2012) *Creating Learning Without Limits*, Berkshire, UK: Open University Press.

Ward, J. (2008) *I Love Dirt*, Boston, MA: Trumpeter Books.

Whinnett, J. (2012) Gifts and occupations: Froebel's gifts (wooden block play) and occupations (construction and workshop experiences) today. In: T. Bruce (ed.) (2012) *Early Childhood Practice: Froebel Today*, London: Sage.

Whitebread, D. and Basilio, M. (2012) The emergence and early development of self-regulation in young children. *Profesorado. Revista de curriculum y formacion del profesorado*. 16(1) (enero–abril 2012). Available online at: www.ugr.es/recfpro/rev161ART2en.pdf (accessed 6 June 2016).

Woods, A. (2016b) *Elemental Play and Outdoor Learning: Young Children's Playful Connections with People, Places and Things*. London: Routledge.

Planning for possibilities with parents

Vicky McEwan

Relationships in the early years are complex because of the emotional factors involved; there are few other professions to which you are compelled and expected to give love, to nurture, and to commit yourself fully to the children and families that you work with.

This chapter will explore the importance of engaging with parents in order to fully involve them when planning possibilities for children's learning and development. It will consider strategies to use when we approach parents in that engagement, considering both the needs of the family and the setting, and how we then develop that engagement into a full, balanced involvement of everyone in the planning process. Through this process, the benefits of parental involvement in planning in relation to the child, family and setting will be discussed drawing on a wide range of current research. It will include a consideration of *at-home* learning and the role of the practitioner in valuing, encouraging, supporting and being actively involved in experiences at home, using a range of strategies including home visits.

The chapter will include encounters that tackle some of the issues around involvement, which can be used for self-reflection. Case studies in the form of encounters in settings with successful parental involvement in planning for possibilities will be used to illustrate strategies to consider. The long-term benefits of sustaining parental relationships will be examined alongside the impact of these on the child, parent, setting and community. The term 'parent' in this chapter should be taken to include those who are in the parenting role for a child, including where a child is cared for by the state.

We already involve parents here

The following encounter reflects a general assumption in many early years settings that by providing parents with a copy of the planning we are 'allowing them' or 'inviting them' to contribute to their child's learning. In looking at how settings work with parents, the taxonomy from the Parents as Partners in Early Learning

---

ENCOUNTER: The planning is on the wall!

An early years adviser for a local authority was carrying out a self-reflection visit to support a day nursery setting, to assess where they were in their provision and to identify strengths and areas for development. It was during this visit that the adviser asked how the setting worked with parents and in particular how parents contributed to their children's learning. The nursery manager replied that planning was available on the notice board for parents to read about what their child would be doing. This was a setting where the quality of both the environment and the practitioners was good, but they were missing a key element in their provision, the parent.

(PPEL) project (DCSF, 2008) can be used as an example of the journey settings need to travel in order to achieve full partnership and triangulation of practice (Wheeler and Connor, 2006).

The PPEL model (DCSF, 2008) starts with *communication*; the setting in the encounter was operating at this level, when they communicated to parents what they were going to be doing with the children each day. At this level an attitudinal change may occur in parents, as they begin to see what their child will be doing and show an interest in the planning that the setting has communicated by reading the notice board each day. The model then requires the practitioner to engage the parent, for example, as parents are looking at the planning, the practitioner could explain it further, ask parents questions about what their child enjoys at home at the moment and use this information to plan for the child in the setting. This step will move the relationship on from communication to the next level of *engagement*. Once engagement has been achieved, behaviour changes will occur in both the practitioner and the parent; the parent at this stage will feel empowered to be part of their child's learning in the setting and the practitioner will begin to see the parent in a new light as a partner in the child's learning journey. At this point the practitioner will need to sustain the dialogue and relationship in order to achieve full involvement of parents in both their child's care and learning in the setting; this *involvement* is seen as the final level in the PPEL taxonomy. At this point we should not become complacent; sustaining the relationship requires respect, inclusivity, great effort and long-term commitment. Parents and settings both have various pressures on their time but the relationship needs time and investment in new projects to prevent it slipping back into engagement, rather than full reciprocal involvement. This requires commitment from the setting as a whole, with leaders and managers that can support their staff teams to build these relationships (see Chapter 8).

In considering what level we are at in the PPEL taxonomy we need to be honest about what really happens in our settings, it may be the case that we are operating at different levels with different parents depending on how comfortable we are with them as individual families, or how long we have known a family for.

We then need to consider if we are being fully inclusive and if there are barriers in moving through the levels from communication to engagement and then to a sustained involvement. Leaders and managers need to observe the practice in their settings and use this as a starting point for dialogue with staff about relationships. Kent (in Woods, 2016: 92) describes a centre's inclusive practice:

> It was central to our practice that we were mindful of the 'dance of reciprocity' (Brazelton *et al.*, 1974) between adult and child and that contingent responsiveness (Gerhardt, 2004) was modelled and embedded in all Centre work and activity. The centrality of reciprocity from a management perspective was seen in the 'conversations' which were encouraged between team members, partners and parents as well as with children in the early stages of Centre development. The pedagogical leadership embraced expectancy and an openness to possibilities (Woods 2013) which meant that the Centre was being built on high quality relationships which recognised the importance of reciprocal communication in supporting and managing change and meeting expectations.

As a result of this, the centre developed early in its life as a place where parents were supported to become observers of their children as they played and interacted with the environment which was provided; parents were included in our planning for the learning and development of their child. We espoused the view that 'babies learn best by playing with the things they find in their world and above all by playing with the familiar people who love them' (DfES 2003: 150). From baby massage to heuristic play sessions, staff modelled and supported parents in 'reading' their baby, to follow their lead and to modify their own language, gaze and 'tone' in response to their child's level of responsiveness. The language of containment and reciprocity provided a lens through which we planned, delivered and reflected upon all centre activity.

The benefits of parental involvement

The benefits of involving parents in their children's learning have long been recognised, (Desforges and Abouchaar (2003), Goldman (2005), Whalley (2007) and Allen (2011)). There are benefits that can be seen for the child; these are not purely benefits in children's cognitive development but the all-round holistic development of the child in both the short and long term. Whitebread and Basilio (2012: 28) have summarized that 'Recent research has shown, for example, that the sensitivity and responsivity of parental interactions with infants may play a significant role in facilitating the organisation of the infant's psychological system necessary for achieving self-regulation'. This closely follows the more established findings of Tizard and Hughes, and Trevarthen. The parent/family, the practitioner and the setting as a whole will benefit from effective parental involvement.

Wheeler and Connor (2006) liken this three-way relationship to a triangle, all parts contribute equally to its strength, however they stress that if one of the three elements is under threat it will have a negative effect on the other two elements. This threat can come in many forms: for the parent it may be anxiety about leaving the child, the development, achievement and outcomes for their child, and worries about work or finances; for the practitioner it can be because they are not supported in the setting with effective supervision; and for the child it can be the stress of separation from their parent.

In discussing reasons why parents participate, Spaggiari explains that this comes from a 'desire to seek opportunities for personal growth or for their children's growth, for meaningful experiences and to both give and receive enrichment and help' (cited in Gandini, 1998a: 106). This makes it clear to us that we are not only adding value to the child's development but the parents' too, in involving parents in planning for possibilities in children's learning we are investing in them as a parent in the context of their family but also as an individual. This is an important factor to consider and perhaps one that we are not always aware of, but by involving parents we are making a difference to the family as a whole, catalyzing the dynamic interplay of Bronfenbrenner's ecological systems model.

This idea of personal growth and empowerment in parents is vital as it has been found that services that involve parents and families fully in decision making and identifying their needs rather than providing things 'for' or doing things 'to' families are most effective, as the change agent is the parent (Sheridan *et al.*, 2004). Swanson *et al.* (2011) found that if practitioners supported parents' self-efficacy then the parent was more able to provide everyday natural learning experiences for their child. This is supported by research by Smith *et al.* (2009) who found that the parents of 2-year-old children attending high quality settings found their parenting skills and relationships with their children were much improved in the time the child attended the setting and that they were able to provide a more stimulating home learning environment.

In order for children to learn effectively they need to feel emotionally secure, and this security comes from the adults and environment around them. They need time and space to form these strong attachments within the setting. They will form these attachments at a quicker rate if they can see that their parent is at ease in the setting and has formed positive, respectful relationships with the staff in the setting and particularly with the child's key person. The role of the key person here is vital in making sure the child feels cherished and that the parent has someone they can talk to about their child (Elfer *et al.*, 2012); for example, sharing things from how their child slept that night to a question they had asked about why birds have wings on the way to the setting that morning. Alongside this communication, however, are layers of emotions that have to be considered, 'the Key Persons approach should help manage these feelings' (Elfer *et al.*, 2012: 35). Managing these emotional relationships is complex and requires a highly skilled practitioner; the encounter in practice sees the challenges settings face in their everyday work.

ENCOUNTER: Do we tell Mum?

An early years adviser walks into a baby room where the three staff are all watching Samar as he holds onto the table. He wants to play with a train that sits on a chair a little too far away for him to reach, so he reaches out and tries to grasp it several times and then looks towards his key person, Cathy, who smiles and says in an encouraging tone 'Go on, you can get it'. He waits, looks and then leaves the security of the table and takes his first tottering steps towards the chair, he grabs the chair and then the train, looking again at Cathy, who along with the other two staff have broken into cheers and applause. He smiles, clearly proud of his achievement. Cathy then looks at the others and says 'Don't tell Mum, she will be upset he walked here first'. The adviser questions this decision but it is clearly a complex situation and one that has over-shadowed Samar's achievement today as the staff agonise over what they should do.

ENCOUNTER: With staff

Retrospective discussion with staff involved in the early implementation of the Children's Centre reveal the threads beginning to develop as to how directing parents to support their children's learning and involvement had to become intentional in our thinking and planning. An early years professional reflected 'were parents really interested in their children's learning or was the Centre viewed just as a safe place to play'? We reminisced on how we were aware that parents' perceptions of their own competence was sometimes poor once their children moved beyond babyhood and that there was a sense of 'waiting' for formal education to start, with many parents expressing the view that their child was 'bored' at home and 'ready for nursery'. We recognised that 'there is an ongoing judgement to be made by practitioners about the balance between activities led by children, and activities led or guided by adults' (EYFS, DfE 2014). We reflected on how the environment was a positive place with planned areas and thought-out opportunities for socialisation but also how we had to gently introduce parents to a deeper engagement with their children's learning through 'sharing our observations with them, suggesting small thinking points, putting information on our display boards and showing consistency (in our own approaches)'. Our Centre statement encouraged parents to allow exploration by highlighting in group publicity that children might get messy and that it did not matter! 'We were also trying to break the mould of parent perceptions of what a Stay and Play session was and that it was not about parents sitting and drinking tea and children doing whatever they liked. But we still wanted the environment to be welcoming and non-judgmental; there was a balance for us between "interfering" and engagement. We wanted to show parents that it was ok to watch their children playing.' This was clearly developed through our heuristic play sessions where children were allowed to explore the materials as they were interested in them

> and parents were encouraged not to direct their children's play but instead to observe their children and to allow the play to develop and reach a natural finishing point without an adult lead.
>
> Staff recalled 'parents asked us to do it again! They became much more open-minded to their child's learning and talked about how they adapted to their children's interests and involvement.'
>
> (Kent, in Woods, 2016a: 94–5)

This is a situation many practitioners will have faced and there is never an easy solution but we must not lose sight of the child and what he has achieved. There are many emotions here experienced by Cathy and the others, first pride and joy, quickly followed by guilt and anxiety. In telling the parent they are concerned she will feel jealousy, perhaps remorse and guilt but in not telling her they fear they are betraying both Samar and his Mum. It is only through an open and honest dialogue with parents that we can begin to unpick these complexities and find a way of working together to appropriately support the child's development and learning. Here we can celebrate Samar's walking and we need to be mindful of sharing *this* news when we might be quicker to 'tell mum' of a biting incident.

It is important that we also consider here children that are looked after by the state, which includes children that are in foster care, and children for whom the state is seeking new parents in the form of adoption. When we consider these children it is vitally important that we work with the team around the child to plan for the child's development and learning. These children have often had very unsettled lives and an early years setting may have been the only constant and therefore their relationship with their key person becomes of paramount importance. The key person here can ensure that others know about what the child is currently interested in, what is of importance to them at present and what explorations they make. In sharing this type of information and seeking dialogue with other professionals we can support the voice of the child and ensure continuity and progression in learning.

The Allen Review of Early Intervention (2011) identifies the need to engage with parents in Early Intervention programmes that will support the 'social and emotional bedrock' (Allen, 2011: xvii) of our future generations. Allen suggests that this support starts long before a child attends school, identifying the needs of children in the womb, in order to give children the best support in life and that this support should then continue with them throughout childhood.

Possibilities of involvement

At-home learning has been identified as a key factor in children's development. Sylva *et al.* (2004) identified that what parents did with their children was more important than who they were. This is a significant finding by Sylva *et al.* (2004) and key to our understanding when working with parents. It tells us that the actions of parents and the provision made for children within the home impact more on children's cognitive development than the parents' socio-economic status and their education level. The research by Sylva *et al.* (2004) identified several experiences that a child can have at home to promote cognitive development. These included experiences such as sharing stories, rhymes, poems and songs and playing with letters, cooking, but also experiences such as going on visits and providing regular opportunities to play with other children. The setting can promote these elements of parent and child activity in a range of ways, which will be explored later in the chapter.

Many early years programmes have parental involvement firmly embedded. The New Zealand Early Years Curriculum of Te Whāriki (1996) has four guiding principles, one of which is Whanau Tangata: Family and Community. The influence of Bronfenbrenner's Ecological Systems Theory (Bronfenbrenner, 1979) and the interplay between the microsystem of family and setting can clearly be seen within the guiding principle of Whanau Tangata. Much can be taken from this way of working by focussing in on how our setting engages with families in a reciprocal way and looking at how we develop and sustain this as a constant in the time a child and family are with us. This begins with home visits prior to a child starting with us, then continues as we provide regular opportunities, both formal and informal, to talk with parents about their child's interests, current lines of enquiry, care needs, holistic development and learning needs.

Home visits are often seen as too time consuming, too risky and not wanted by families; however, the visit can be viewed as one of the first steps in achieving a balanced reciprocal relationship with parents. Home visits should have a clear focus that is decided upon by the setting and the parent prior to the visit. A phone conversation about the visit should not only deal with the practicalities of the visit but set out what you as the practitioner hope to achieve: meeting the child and parent, finding out what they enjoy doing together, gathering information about the child and the family, providing an opportunity to talk with parents about what they hope they and their child will gain from attending the setting and finally to ensure a smooth transition into the setting. It is vital that parents feel listened to and that you convey to them that you see them as experts in knowledge about their child. Simple strategies such as taking a camera with you and photographing the child with their family and then ensuring this is displayed on a welcome board in the entrance hall alongside all the other families creates an ethos of 'this place is for me and my child, we are welcome here, we are part of what happens here'. If you have made notes about what a child enjoys doing and then have planned for this to take place on their first day then it communicates the message that you have listened and responded to what parents have shared. This in turn is likely to increase the likelihood of them sharing more with you in the future, thus taking the first steps in shared planning for the child.

In the Te Whāriki curriculum the documentation of children's learning in Learning Stories (Carr, 2001) demonstrates the triangulation of parents, children and practitioners as they actively discuss the learning together (Cowie and Carr, 2009). Many settings develop wonderful learning journeys that could become a catalyst for engaging parents; they should be encouraged to access them at any time, share them with their children, contribute to them on an ongoing basis and in a range of ways and feel a shared ownership over them with the child and practitioner.

Parents' involvement in the documentation within the Reggio Emilia approach also contributes to our understanding of the possibilities afforded to us in involving parents in children's learning. Within the Reggio Emilia approach pedagogical documentation is shared in a reflective way with parents. It can be used as a lens through which the parent can come to have deeper understanding of their child; this deeper understanding will lead to a parent who is more knowledgeable and confident to both provide for more learning opportunities at home and contribute fully to learning in the setting. In discussing negotiated learning in Reggio Emilia settings, Forman and Fyfe tell us that: '[Parents'] observations, combined with the teachers' observations, can lead to an even deeper understanding of children's thoughts, feelings and dispositions' (1998: 252).

This is echoed in Woods' (2016b: 20) research with parents attending an outdoor garden group where the parents were asked 'What were the reasons for joining Little Muddy Boots? (A parent and toddler group for under-fives in a large enclosed garden), and secondly, 'What do you think [your children] have enjoyed most and how do you know this'? They replied:

- I wanted my daughter to learn about nature and learn that getting messy/dirty can be fun;

- To give my children outdoors natural play fostering creativity and love of outdoors; [later response]–we often continue activities at home (harvesting, planting, watering, cutting Mr Grass hair);

- Being amongst other children and muddy play as my son talks about it at home;

- [second response]–yes, we keep things we have made at home to tell other family members about what we have done;

- To enjoy the outdoors together with my daughter in a more structured way; to help her learn and develop; E also loves taking things she's made home to show Daddy;

- Gain more experiences that are age appropriate for 20 month twins to follow up at home;

- Yes, P has enjoyed telling his Daddy about muddy boots especially tractor painting.

Here we have a mixture of parents wanting to re-visit early memories and the enjoyment of playing outdoors, as well as sharing and re-learning gardening habits, and for some, support in developing new skills with their children. I watched story stick making, stick weaving and winding, watering seeds and young plants and harvesting a variety of beans, and witnessed the parents enjoying this time as much as the children; they were probably less wet and muddy than the little ones' frequent trips between water butt and mud kitchen.

If staff in these settings have this deeper understanding alongside parents, not only will the home learning environment be improved but the setting can personalise the setting's learning environment to the child. The Encounter: George asks a question demonstrates how dialogue and planning together can enhance a child's experiences. It involves George, a 4-year-old attending a day nursery full time. The nursery operates a target child planning system where each key person talks about one of their children each week in the planning meeting through involving the child's dad in this encounter many more possibilities were opened up as many of the experiences planned for would not have been possible without parental support and engagement.

ENCOUNTER: George asks a question

He continues to be interested in connecting everything together using string and wool; he joined together the tables, door handles and made a massive web that we eventually had to cut our way out of. He turned all the bikes upside down outside and spun the wheels to watch them turn, he was really excited about it but it caused problems when others wanted to ride them.

He asked many questions about rotation this week:

'Why does the water go round and round and then down . . . where does it go?' exploring water washing hands.

'Why do the wheels on that car all turn round and round but those ones twist round too?' observing the wheels on the cars and which way they were being turned as a car parked.

'Why does the roundabout go round but stay still, it's not like a Frisbee that goes round and moves . . . wheels go round and move too, it is just there but it won't move over?' pushing the roundabout in the park.

The staff came up with a detailed plan of action for the following week to support both his rotation and connecting schema. The plan included asking his dad (a plumber) to come in and remove the waste pipe in the sink so he could watch the water pass through the plug hole into the bucket.

His dad was pleased to come in and removed the pipe, and George and the other children really enjoyed seeing water gush through. This led to more questions from George about where the water normally went if the pipe was on, which his dad helped him to answer by following all the manhole covers and drainage system through the garden, out into the road and eventually a drive to the local sewage works to see where the water would eventually go. Dad also went along with him and his key person to a local garage to watch tyres being changed, to see the fixed and moving parts of the wheel.

ENCOUNTER: Come to the party!

In one of the most deprived areas of the country a reception class is excited that they are having a party to welcome Ted the Going Home Bear to their class. For once nearly every child is present and they are involved in getting things ready for their parents who are coming at 2.30. They have written and taken home invites for parents, grandparents, other key adults and younger siblings; they have made sandwiches and cut up vegetable sticks and fruit; and they have put together goodie bags for younger siblings. The parents gradually start to arrive and their children quickly involve them in planned activities and games. For those children that don't have anyone coming to the party, support staff have been recruited from around the school to be their guest. The teacher has carefully engineered the whole event to feel welcoming but it has a clear focus on drawing the parents through the door and giving their children time to tell them about what they have been doing.

A key strategy to building relevant and supportive experiences for the child both at home and in the setting is to provide parents and practitioners time with the child together, as demonstrated in 'George asks a question' when the key person and dad went with George to the garage. This can be achieved in many ways with a little creativity and time; the dividends of this are well worth the investment as it sustains the dialogue, provides opportunities to talk about the child and the family at a deeper level, and provides opportunity to observe and plan together.

Home visits are often restricted to a child's transition into the setting but some settings very successfully continue these and provide them throughout the child's time, perhaps at key points, for example, moving to a new group within the same setting. The visits can have a focus such as taking along a story sack to share, the practitioner can then model how to use it and leave it behind for the child and family to continue to share afterwards. Stay and play or open door sessions are another key approach to being able to spend time with the child and family. This can be very successful if planned at the start or end of the day and if parents are given advanced warning that it is happening so they are able to arrange time off work. A very helpful way of starting this off was observed in a reception classroom.

This encounter was built upon by sending thank–you letters and then extending an invite to come every Friday afternoon to have tea and celebrate what they had been doing that week. The teacher and classroom support staff would ensure that each Friday those parents that came were welcomed and given the opportunity to talk to them. Some parents came weekly and this clearly had a positive impact on the child's attendance and the parents' involvement in their child's learning as they continued projects at home or borrowed resources to use at home.

At the end of this chapter provocations will encourage you to consider how you can develop these regular opportunities for parents and practitioners to spend time together with children.

Challenges that can be faced when we work with parents

Parenting is difficult and it is only once you become a parent that you begin to really understand the complexities of the parent/child relationship and the daily challenges that parents face. In order to build relationships with practitioners, parents look for certain qualities and attitudinal behaviours from the practitioners that they meet (Wheeler and Connor, 2006). These include; patience, recognising that parents have a load to carry, just being there and being non-judgemental, listening carefully, signposting and giving hope. Many practitioners naturally have these qualities but some such as signposting can only be acquired through developing knowledge and experience.

It is vitally important that practitioners are trained in how to work with parents and that settings have detailed policies and guidance on parental partnerships. Many training programmes at all levels only briefly cover this aspect of working with parents and when they do they tend to include the surface-level elements, such as having a policy on parental involvement, rather than the elements Wheeler and Connor (2006) tell us are needed such as listening and giving hope. Leaders and managers are key here in mentoring and coaching staff to develop these skills needed to work with parents.

One barrier that faces many early years practitioners when trying to engage parents in their children's learning is cultural diversity and the challenges of having many different cultures and languages represented in our settings. The communities we work in are a rich tapestry of languages and cultures that can be used to provide a wealth of learning opportunities but it can also be an obstacle *for us* in achieving involvement from parents. When working with families that do not speak English, we need to consider the possibilities this gives us for celebrating diversity. Encounter: Midwinter festival explores diversity and a setting's creative and innovative approach to bringing together their community.

ENCOUNTER: Midwinter festival

A pre-school in a deprived area of a large town is celebrating a midwinter festival. They have decided to do this rather than a Christmas Party this year as many of their families do not celebrate Christmas. All families have been invited to come along and bring a dish of food from their culture to share. As you walk into the room you smell the wonderful aroma of foods from different cultures, you hear the chatter as parents and practitioners sit together at a large table talking, sharing experiences and you see the children playing together, running, laughing, shouting, having fun. The manager sits back and watches what is unfolding around her; this is greater than anything she was hoping for and her battle with the committee over health and safety and food hygiene regulations is a distant memory.

The families in this encounter did not all speak English but together they were constructing a valuable learning experience for the children. The children were learning so much about their own and other cultures, they learned the names of the foods they were trying in the language of where the food originated from, they learned how to get along with others in a social situation and developed their sense of belonging. The practitioners when reflecting on the celebration were proud of what they had achieved that day and they also benefited from it in the long term as the relationships that were forged that day were developed. The impact on individual children was evident as parents felt more at ease in the setting and they moved from communicating to deep level engagement about their children's learning. The language barriers were still there but parents and practitioners attempted simple phrases in each other's languages and together they communicated successfully.

All parents and families are different and we will only be able to work effectively with them if we find out how they work and take time to understand the complexities and challenges that they have in their relationships. Darling (1999) describes parenting as 'a complex activity that includes many specific behaviours that work individually and together to influence child outcomes'. Much of the literature in relation to working with parents makes reference to parenting styles. Research by Scott et al. (2012) found that a negative parenting style with harsh behaviour management and lacking in consistency was clearly associated with anti-social behaviour. It is clear to all educators that dispositions to learning are the key to long-term academic achievement and therefore parenting style is a key contributing factor that we need to consider. One of the key elements of parenting style is parental responsiveness (Barimund, 1991). Parental responsiveness is demonstrated by how emotionally warm the parent is with their child, how supportive they are of their child's individual needs and how attuned they are to their child. The second element to consider in relation to parenting styles is parental 'demandingness' or behaviour control (Barimund, 1991), which captures elements such as how parents supervise children's play and how they manage their child's behaviour. If we take time to observe these elements in the parent/child relationship and sensitively discuss these elements of parenting with parents we will be able to support them to develop their parenting skills and thus create opportunities for involvement in children's learning both at home and in the setting.

Research exploring parenting style (Barimund, 1991) indicates that an authoritative parenting style is most effective in supporting children's development and learning, as these parents are both responsive and demanding. This is displayed as they support their child in an emotionally warm relationship but with clear boundaries.

The dad in the Encounter: Look at the aeroplanes Daddy! displayed all the characteristics of the authoritative parent: he was responsive, demonstrated in his warm, clear affection and attunement to his daughter but he was also demanding in his clear behavioural expectations. The learning that came from the encounter with the aeroplanes was so very rich in possibilities but if you had asked that

ENCOUNTER: Look at the aeroplanes Daddy!

At a busy airport boarding gate a young dad and his daughter are looking out of the window at the aeroplane. The dad is crouched down and his daughter leans close to him, resting her elbows on his knees. He explains how they will get onto the aeroplane and what it will sound like when the engines start; he responds to her questions and comments, demonstrating many of the elements of sustained shared thinking. She bangs on the window with her hands, he removes her hands placing them in his and asks her to stop, she smiles at him and goes back to leaning on his knees. They continue their discussion about the aeroplane and their holiday, unaware of other dramas unfolding around them and totally focussed on each other.

ENCOUNTER: Michael's mum

On 29 June, the weather was challenging, pretty torrential rain throughout but I have noted that Michael has particularly enjoyed today. Often running and slipping, he has sprawled in the mud many times; his sleeves are wet, his face is covered in mud splash and he has giggled and shouted as the children have tried to catch water off the canopy. Parents were called early that session as the children became quite cold.

Michael has attended 5/6 sessions and this evidence does not fully show the impact of forest school on his social and emotional development. It is only when reflecting with his mum that we can see what this experience meant to him.

One of the leaders asked his mum:

'How do you think it has benefited Michael?'

She said: 'freedom to do things without . . . worrying. He is sometimes not very good in large groups. Working in a small group has really helped him talk about forest school. He would go every single day. I think it has brought him on, brought on his confidence. He is more relaxed in preschool.'

The leader responds:

'I've heard his voice in the forest more.'

Later his mum adds:

'When we are out, he is always asking "what tree is this?" He had a newt all week, let it crawl all over him, talked to it. Everything outdoors, he is interested. We've never built houses with sticks before, never done this before forest school. He knows nettles and dock leaves, telling his brother to hold his hands up high. (Brother is 2). He is choosing a lot more and will talk about forest school.'

Mum has seen an impact in Michael's voice, confidence, knowledge, well-being, autonomy; this is powerful, and she so enjoyed telling us this. The leaders noted his speaking in the woods and they reflected that there had been concerns over his

> speech development. Confidence to speak in groups of children often hides the actual ability to converse and share dialogue and it is wonderful to have been a part in his positive well-being in the woods. Sharing this with his mum was a very powerful event and will have encouraged her to become more engaged in the outdoors with her children.

dad to talk about learning and teaching he may not have realised that what he and his daughter had engaged in that time at the boarding gate was anything other than chatting.

To many parents teaching their child and creating possibilities for learning comes quite naturally but for others, with different parenting styles at home, learning and involvement in children's learning in the setting can be limited by their levels of confidence, responsiveness and demandingness. This is clearly a challenge for early years educators but one that can be overcome by providing opportunities, both formal and informal, to talk about learning and qualities of effective teaching. One such opportunity was narrated in the previous encounter (Woods, 2015: 99). At the end of the first series of sessions at a new forest school, parents were invited to an informal evening to chat about the experience.

Successful relationships with endless possibilities

We have already discussed in this chapter many of the possibilities that can be afforded by engaging with parents in planning for children's learning and development but let us now turn our attention to how we sustain that relationship. Often we find that we introduce new initiatives and they are successful for a while but then they gradually fade away as we turn our attention to the next project. We should not allow that to happen in the practices we establish to support us in planning for possibilities with parents. Whalley discusses the need for a sustainable approach to embed the 'Parents' Involvement in their Children's Learning' (PICL) Programme developed by Pen Green:

> [Staff] have to develop a shared language with parents and a shared under-standing about how children develop and how children learn, both at home and in the nursery. It is vital that staff understand parents' own theories about the development of their child and their child's learning at home. It is also essential that nursery staff share with parents their theoretical and practice-based understanding of the children drawn from their own observations of the children in the nursery setting . . . working in this way produces outcomes that transform children's life chances.
>
> (Whalley, 2007: 201)

It is clear that sustaining this type of relationship takes time and a confident, highly skilled practitioner but the long lasting benefits to the child, parent and society as a whole are clearly worth the effort and commitment of both time and money. Its success was enhanced by the joint use of technology; parents and practitioners would video their children and in dialogic activity would jointly observe, reflect, stop the film, interpret and consider next steps. Parental insight and practitioner scrutiny and mediation cannot be under-estimated for its value.

> A systematic review of recent studies of parental influence on self-regulation among pre-schoolers and primary aged children has identified a number of characteristic parenting dimensions and behaviours which have consistently found to be related to metacognitive and motivational aspects of self-regulated learning (Pino-Pasternak & Whitebread, 2010).
>
> (Whitebread and Basilio, 2012: 16)

Sustaining the relationships leads to full participation and reciprocity. We need to continually develop new strategies to communicate and work with parents. We need to look at opportunities that arise from the advances of technology to have a dialogue with parents about how their child develops and constructs new knowledge, not only in the setting but at home and in the community. Learning should be viewed as an active social process that can be supported by parents who are attuned to their child, and practitioners who are enablers of that learning.

We can also consider the role of the community here. The Pre-Schools and Infant Toddler Centres of Reggio Emilia operate a system of community-based management that aims to support, enhance and develop positive interactions and communications between the settings, families and the local communities in which they are based. They see this triangulation as the key to the holistic educational experience children encounter in their settings. We have a history in this country of voluntary managed early years settings (pre-schools and playgroups) but many of them have disappeared due to demographic and economic change and demands. This is a great shame; we need to exploit the opportunities our communities offer in the way they do in Reggio Emilia and this can be done by all types of providers by having a community/parent forum where interested parties can come together to plan projects, discuss opportunities and share principles and philosophy. The Bristol street play project is a good contemporary example. In discussing the participation of parents in Reggio Emilia settings Spaggiari tells us that this interaction can 'promote a new style of political commitment that favours childhood' (cited in Gandini, 1998b: 111).

In this chapter we have explored many aspects of parental involvement. We have seen the clear benefits that this can have to the child's holistic development and 'life chances' (Whalley, 2007: 201). Parental partnership needs to be balanced and parents empowered to make changes themselves to be most effective and offer possibilities in learning. To conclude, we draw together the many ideas and reflect on the impact planning for possibilities with parents can have on our families if we fully engage them through the words of a parent of a child in a Reggio Emilia pre-school who talks about her place and identity in the school's community:

> Perhaps this sense of place and belonging to a community based on openness, trust and respect has been their greatest gift to me . . . and to us as a family.
>
> (Laesk, 2001: 47)

Provocations

- At what stage of the PPEL taxonomy are you operating at with the parents in your setting?

- Are all parents fully included in their children's learning and development? Do they have regular opportunities, both formal and informal, to contribute to their children's learning in the setting?

- How do you support parents to understand the value of the experiences they give their children at home?

- How do you encourage parents to engage their children at home in the types of activities identified by Sylva et al. (2004) that support their cognitive development?

- What materials would support parents to provide these types of experiences for their child?

- What small steps could you take to enhance the possibilities that are afforded by engaging parents?

- How do you currently work with the community? What possibilities does your community have for closer dialogue and working?

References

Allen, G. (2011) *Early Intervention: The Next Steps*, London: Cabinet Office.

Barimund, D. (1991) The influence of parenting style on adolescent competence and substance use. *Journal of Early Adolescence*, 11(1): 56–95.

Bronfenbrenner, U. (1979) *The Ecology of Human Development: Experiments by Nature and Design*, London: Harvard University Press.

Carr, M. (2001) *Assessment in Early Childhood Settings: Learning Stories*, London: Paul Chapman.

Cowie, B. and Carr, M. (2009) The consequences of socio-cultural assessment. In: A. Anning, J. Cullen and M. Fleer (eds). *Early Education: Society and culture*, 2nd edn, London: Sage.

Darling, N. (1999) Parenting style and its correlates, *ERIC Digest*. EDO-PS-99–3. Available online at: www.ericdigests.org/1999–4/parenting.htm (accessed 30 November 2011).

DCSF (Department for Children, Schools and Families) (2008) *Parents Partners in Early Learning*, Nottingham, UK: HMSO.

Desforges, C. and Abouchaar, A. (2003) *The impact of parental involvement, parental support and family education on pupil achievements and adjustment: A literature review*, Research Report 433. Nottingham, UK: Department for Education and Skills.

DfE (Department for Education) (2014) *Statutory Framework for the Early Years Foundation Stage*. Available at: https://www.gov.uk/government/uploads/system/uploads/attachment_data/file/335504/EYFS_framework_from_1_September_2014_with_clarification_note.pdf (accessed 4 May, 2015).

DfES (Department for Education and Skills). (2003) *Birth to Three Matters. A Framework to Support Children in their Earliest Years*. DfES Publishing: Nottingham.

Elfer, P., Goldschmied, E. and Selleck, D. (2012) *Key Persons in the Early Years*, 2nd edn, Oxford: David Fulton.

Forman, G. and Fyfe, B. (1998) Negotiated learning through design, documentation, and discourse. In: C. Edwards, L. Gandini and G. Forman (eds). *The Hundred Languages of Children*, 2nd edn, London: Ablex.

Gandini, L. (1998a) The Community-Teacher Partnership in the Governance of the Schools. In: C. Edwards, L. Gandini and G. Forman (eds). *The Hundred Languages of Children*, 2nd edn, London: Ablex.

Gandini, L. (1998b) Projected curriculum constructed through documentation – Progettazoine. In: C. Edwards, L. Gandini and G. Forman (eds). *The Hundred Languages of Children*, 2nd edn, London: Ablex.

Goldman, R. (2005) *Fathers' Involvement in their Children's Education*, London: NFPI.

Kent, J. (2016a) Chapter 6. Embracing levels of involvement. In: Woods, A. (ed.). *Examining Levels of Involvement in the Early Years. Engaging with Children's Possibilities*. London: David Fulton.

Laesk, J. (2001) Sam's invisible extra gear – a parent's view. In: Abbot, L. and Nutbrown, C. (eds). *Experiencing Reggio Emilia: Implications for Pre-school Provision*. Maidenhead, UK: Open University Press.

Ministry of Education (1996) *Te Whariki*, Wellington, NZ: Learning Media Limited.

Rinaldi, C. (2006) *In Dialogue with Reggio Emilia*, London: Routledge.

Scott, S., Doolan, M., Beckett, C., Harry, S. and Cartwright, S. (2012) *How is parenting style related to child antisocial behaviour? Preliminary findings from the Helping Children Achieve Study*. Research Report 185a. London: Department for Education.

Sheridan, S., Warnes, E., Cowan, R., Schemm, A. and Clarke, B. (2004) *Family-centred positive psychology: Focussing on strengths to build student success*, Educational Psychology Papers and Publications, Paper 5, Nebraska: University of Nebraska-Lincoln, Department of Educational Psychology. Available online at: www.digitalcommons.unl.edu/cgi/view content.cgi?article=1004&context=edpsychpapers (accessed 12 July 2012).

Smith, R., Pudon, S., Schneider, V., La Valle, I., Wollny, I., Owen, R., Bryson, C., Mathers, S., Sylva, K. and Lloyd, E. (2009) *Early education pilot for two year old children evaluation.* DCSF Research Report 134. London: Department for Children, Schools and Families.

Swanson, J., Raab, M. and Dunst, C. (2011) Strengthening family capacity to provide young children everyday natural learning. *Journal of Early Childhood Research*, 9(1): 66–80.

Sylva, K., Melhuish, E., Sammons, P., Siraj-Blatchford, I. and Taggart, B. (2004) *The Effective Provision of Pre-school Education (EPPE) Project: Final report*, London: DfES and Institute of Education, University of London.

Whalley, M. (2007) *Involving Parents in their Children's Learning*, 2nd edn, London: Paul Chapman Press.

Wheeler, H. and Connor, J. (2006) *Parents' Early Years and Learning*, London: National Children's Bureau.

Whitebread, D. and Basilio, M. (2012) The emergence and early development of self-regulation in young children. *Profesorado. Revista de curriculum y formacion del profesorado,* 16(1) (enero-abril 2012). Available online at: www.ugr.es/recfpro/rev161ART2en.pdf (accessed 6 June 2016).

Woods, A. (ed.) (2015) *The Characteristics of Effective Learning. Creating and Capturing the Possibilities in the Early Years.* London: David Fulton.

Woods, A. (ed.) (2016a) *Examining Levels of Involvement in the Early Years. Engaging with children's possibilities.* London: David Fulton.

Exploring the possibilities of children's voice

Moira Moran

In this chapter we will turn our attention to the child's voice and how it can be foregrounded in our provision. Before beginning it may be worthwhile to remind ourselves of the rationale for this discussion. The context for considering children's voice in planning has been firmly set by the United Nations Convention on the Rights of the Child (UNCRC), the 54 Articles of which were ratified by the United Kingdom in 1991. Of particular relevance to this chapter is Article 12, which states that signatories

> shall assure to the child who is capable of forming his or her own views the right to express those views freely in all matters affecting the child, the views of the child being given due weight in accordance with the age and maturity of the child.

> (UN, 1989)

Following the death of Victoria Climbié in 2000, Laming's report (2003) recommended listening to children whenever appropriate in issues of safeguarding and child protection. His recommendations fed into the Children Act (2004) and the five outcomes of the Every Child Matters agenda (DfES, 2003), which were drawn up by children and young people themselves. The active participation of children and young people in forming this policy exemplifies the UNCRC expectation and requirement on governments that the views of young stakeholders be respected and addressed in policy making that concerns them.

The DfES commissioned a major piece of research into the status of listening and consultation with young children (Clark *et al.*, 2003), demonstrating the commitment of the then government to this field, and leading to a national training programme and materials (Lancaster and Broadbent, 2003, Lancaster and Kirby, 2010); local strategy and setting practice developed to incorporate a rights–based approach and listening culture (Moran, 2006).

Over the years since 1991, the powerful UNCRC commitments, reflected in changes to law and national and local policy, have fed into practice with even the youngest children, to the extent that it would be hard to imagine our time with little children when we do not interact with, relate to and observe them in order to know their interests and preferences – to hear their voice. However, careful reading of the whole of Article 12 demonstrates that listening to children is only a part of our obligation. A young disabled child said, 'People let me speak and say what I feel because they have to, but then ignore what I say because it's not what they want to do' (Crow *et al.*, 2008: 10).

We need to find ways to 'give due weight' to children's views, and to ensure that they are acted on. In other words, the Article asks us to afford children the opportunity to be active participants in decisions and plans made within their setting. For some adults, this may be a challenging idea, and the challenge can arise from our view of the *unique* child. It is likely that few of us today still hold the views of our forebears that children should be seen and not heard, but do we hold the view of a child as innocent, dependent and vulnerable (Moss and Petrie, 2002), or do we see the child as 'rich in potential, strong, powerful, competent and, most of all, connected to adults and other children' (Malaguzzi, 1993: 10)? This question is important because our view of the child influences our view of the role of the adult in relation to the child, and affects our pedagogical choices.

We know and understand that communication takes place between mother and child before birth. Hart (1992) identified the child's *participation* as starting from birth when interaction between the parent and the child as an individual begins. Adult responses to children's communication through cries and gestures vary from family to family and are culturally influenced, and Hart proposes that 'through these early negotiations, even in infancy, children discover the extent to which their own voices influence the course of events in their lives' (1992: 4).

> It is apparent that the human infant is interested in and responsive to the emotions and the behavior of others. Trevarthen (1977) showed that infants as young as two months of age show a different response to someone who speaks to them than to someone else in the room who remains silent.
>
> (Smidt, 2013: 39)

Immediately the process of co-construction can begin if there are attentive and responsive adults on hand to tune into and interpret the child's message and if the child is perceived as already a social being, active and competent in their own ideas and decisions.

In this chapter I will discuss how we can tune into the voice of all our children in the setting, including the youngest babies, and those who, because of particular circumstances, struggle to make their voice heard. Parents and colleagues can help us in this. I will consider how, once we have listened to the child's voice, we can act as their advocate, to ensure that their voice is heard. I will finish by proposing that, even with these young children, we can progress from consulting with them to enabling their participation in the decisions which affect them, to the benefit of us all.

Tuning into children's voices

In settings, practitioners who respect children's rights will observe their actions, tuning into all their ways of communicating their preferences, interests and fascinations. Clark and Moss (2011) describe the Mosaic Approach through which children make photographs and maps that are linked to interviews and observations to elicit children's views. Mortimer (2007) describes an approach which allows the full involvement and participation of the youngest children and babies through sustained narrative observations of interactions between the baby and all staff involved, which are then reflected on by the team. Tuning into children's voices can often be witnessed through best practice.

How valuable this sensitive approach is to the individual preferences of each child, and how skilled Chell is in hearing their voice. Her offering of the activity takes time, but the result is that each child has an experience tailored to their personal interest or lack of interest in that particular activity at that particular time. Priya may want to join in tomorrow, and Jacob almost certainly will be ready to build on the experience of today. What can Mitch be offered next to allow him to explore his fascination with sensory experience and develop his mastery of materials? Chell's provision is very different from the one where every child in turn is taken to the creative area to perform the planned activity of the day, as if on a conveyor-belt. In a similar, but longer term Encounter ('Rosie's Treasure Blanket') we can see how a grandmother learns alongside her granddaughter's exploration with a treasure basket and the non–verbal signals given by the baby. Various photographs of each stage have been shared with her mother to support the ongoing interest in objects.

ENCOUNTER: Choice in the baby room

In the baby room Chell is offering a sensory activity to the small group of sitting, non-mobile children. To do this she approaches each baby individually, sits next to them, squirts some baby lotion on her own hand and shows it to the baby, gently saying their name and inviting them to touch her outstretched hand.

Priya turns her head away. Chell says 'Not today, Priya? I can see how busy you are with that shaker' and moves away.

Mitch immediately bangs Chell's hand with his own, and she responds to his preference for splashy, vigorous play, both of them laughing at the squelchy, spattery results when Mitch has lotion on his own hands and claps them together with as much force as he can muster.

Jacob is more tentative, initially touching Chell's hand with just one finger. In a quiet voice she talks to him, smiling encouragingly when he looks at her face. Chell is patient and takes the lead from Jacob as he progresses to smoothing both of Chell's hands with his own, and eventually holds out his own open hands looking at the lotion bottle as a signal to her to put lotion on his hands.

ENCOUNTER: Rosie's treasure basket

As soon as Rosie could independently sit, she was offered a basket of objects. At first her choices of objects were determined by those she could hold and mouth; they were the larger objects. A few weeks on, she chose those small enough to pass from hand to hand as well as to her mouth; she was beginning her first teeth. Rosie then showed us she chose an object for each hand which could bang together, clearly discarding those too big for one hand and another in the second hand or that did not make a satisfying noise. Currently she is more likely to use both hands to turn over objects carefully to look at them from different angles. Always, at the end of her chosen time to play, she leaves the objects, looks up, lifts her arms as if to say 'time for a change, pick me up'.

As Brown (in Woods, 2015:107) suggests:

> When working with babies, very young or non-vocal children, it is vitally important that we as adults are tuned into their emerging needs and interests as they may not express themselves verbally. Children show us their thinking most commonly and uninhibitedly in their freely chosen play. In their play, babies and children may ask questions and express their ideas and feelings with their bodies, through their facial expressions, sounds, body language, actions and gestures as they interact and engage with the world around them using all of their senses. Movement can be seen as thought in action and as such allows thinking to become visible to observant others. Piaget (1983) was among the first to recognise organised and repeated behaviour patterns or cognitive structures in children under the age of 5, which are manifest through children's movement and actions. He termed this as 'scheme of thought' or 'schemas of action' and saw thought as consisting of the internalisation of these schemas.

A perception of each child as competent in the eyes of the practitioner and parent empowers all children to have a voice. Careful attention will need to be employed in order to hear the voice of those children who struggle to make their voice heard. This applies to children with additional needs of all kinds and, again, should include the voice of parents to ensure the fullest possible view of the child. Some children may be isolated by language (delayed development or a first language other than that of the setting), culture, faith or ethnicity, gender, ability or disability. Some children present as quiet within the setting and avoid being recipients of attention, preferring the background to centre stage, whereas others appear to thrive on attention, often engaging with adults and peers. It will be important to consider all of these individualities, since 'An unequal spread of justice will damage the people and cause pain' (Zephaniah, cited in Lane 2008: xv).

Ryan (2005) elaborates on this point through her analysis of observations of children involved in free play. She suggests that various characteristics of children in play (gender in the case of her particular study) can confer on or deny children power as social agents within their group. If we recognise this possibility, we can be alert to it in our observations, and, if and when necessary, we can discuss it with the children themselves. Appropriately raising the children's awareness of dominance and power within their interactions will promote equity within the group, ensuring that hearing the voice of all children is the responsibility of all members of the group, not of the adults alone. Löfdahl (in Brooker and Edwards, 2010: 124) reminds us of our current 'view of children's agency which affirms that children are co-constructers in their own development and participants in societal processes, and thus are able to influence and change structures in their environment.' Edwards *et al.* (Ibid.: 150) add:

> The teacher's task in this situation is to 'know about the possibilities of his or her own pedagogical activity, to use these sensibly and thus raise to a new level the activity, consciousness [and personality] of his or her charges'.
>
> (Davydov, 1995: 17)

Children with Special Educational Needs (SEN) may have a particular member of staff who works closely with them, often in a one-to-one relationship, and so this skilled and knowledgeable person is in an ideal position to represent the voice of that child and family, and to act as the child's advocate; however, that does not exclude other members of staff from making a valuable contribution, in the usual team approach. Inclusive practice is good practice, and good practice is inclusive. Consequently, although a designated practitioner may have detailed knowledge of the child, and specific skills to support them, a truly inclusive team will all contribute their piece of knowledge in order to build up a full picture of the child, how they engage, where they engage, and who and what they engage with (Casey, 2010). There is no magic trick for listening to the voice of these children: we all have the skills. It is the case though, that for some children we may need some extra help from a knowledgeable other, and we may need to listen a bit harder.

ENCOUNTER: Chantelle and the blanket

Julie is a portage worker, home visiting Chantelle, a 3-year-old girl with severe and complex learning and physical disabilities. Today, Julie has brought an insulation blanket, the kind issued to marathon runners, and she lays Chantelle on it, and then gently moves the blanket close to her head so that it rustles and shines close to her face. Chantelle curls her big toe on one foot, and her mum, Fran, and Julie acknowledge this sign of her enjoyment of the new sensations. Julie offers to take a blanket into nursery, so that Chantelle can continue enjoying this new experience in the setting.

The close relationship between Julie and Fran in Encounter: Chantelle and the blanket has resulted in a powerful partnership that interweaves Fran's knowledge of Chantelle's communication of interests and enjoyment with Julie's expertise in the field of Early Years SEN provision. The close relationship between Julie, Fran and Chantelle's key worker at nursery will facilitate the sharing of this knowledge to support the staff in tuning into Chantelle's unique communication. They, in turn, will be able to observe and retell their experiences of offering the blanket to Chantelle, and so contribute their particular perspective to the combined understanding of Chantelle, and best provision for her.

Ensuring the child's voice is heard

Hearing children's voices can prove difficult in busy settings, when the practicalities of the smooth running of the day have to be considered, and when external voices, in the form of policies, frameworks and outcomes, may seem so much louder than those of the individual child. This can lead to routine and planning that dominates provision in an adult-led rather than child-centred approach. If this is the case, then the voice of the child, although listened to, is not always heard. It is here that the role of the key person becomes of prime importance, establishing the vital relationship, attuned to the child and family and engaged with all parties for the best outcomes for the child.

Lizzie, see Encounter: Custard!, was determined to analyse an incident. She feels she is a kind practitioner, with the children's best interests at heart. She works in a nursery which prides itself on fostering children's choices and voice. On reflection, she realises that the issue here is greater than simply listening to children, that she has to ensure that she enables their voice to be heard, and that sometimes that

---

ENCOUNTER: Custard!

Tyrone is new to the nursery, admitted at age 2 following a family relocation. At the end of his first week his key person, Lizzie, is keen to talk to his dad about how well he has settled. Among other things, they discuss meal times, and Lizzie recounts how much he is enjoying meals, except for custard, which he always refuses.

'That's strange' says Tyrone's dad. 'He loves custard at home!'

The two continue to discuss the custard mystery, until eventually it is solved. It is the nursery practice to ask the children if they want custard with their pudding and, if they do, to put on an apron to protect their clothes. Tyrone dislikes the feel of the stiff PVC aprons, and so has quickly decided to forego his favourite custard to avoid the apron. With dad's agreement, Lizzie decides that Tyrone will have custard without an apron. The conversation is subsequently opened up to other parents and children.

depends on the questions which are asked. Consequently she asked other children and their parents about the meal routines, allowing their voices also to be heard. Lizzie learned that few parents minded about messy clothes, but that they all valued the setting's practice of allowing children to make choices about food, and to feed themselves. She reported this to her managers and the apron policy was abandoned. In this one small area of provision, Lizzie had 'given due weight' to the voice of the child.

Sometimes the dominant voice comes from outside the setting, and is that of local or national frameworks or policies. Although early years guidance generally has the concept of the unique child at their heart, they can sometimes become more rigid in the interpretation or implementation than they were intended to be. Concerns to achieve standards of high quality and to meet requirements can become the dominant discourse. This can be the case particularly for those in positions of leadership and management, and for reasons that will be explored in Chapter 8. It is important, however, to ensure that a balance is maintained between a focus on predetermined and measurable outcomes and on the possibilities of what matters and is meaningful to *these* children *now*. By knowing what is important and relevant to them, and by being confident to propose and justify that on their behalf, we become advocates for them, and represent their voice when decisions are being made. We ensure their voice is heard. This is not always an easy position to be in.

ENCOUNTER: Michael's writing

Michael will soon transfer to school and his key worker, Sadia, is feeling the pressure. Michael is a 'typical boy' and though his physical and social profile is high, he has barely progressed in the area of literacy since his admission to the nursery. Now Michael's parents and the nursery leader are suggesting more formal work in this area, to help him catch up with his peers. Sadia knows that Michael loves stories, and shows an interest in letters and print, but he is reluctant to mark-make or attempt to write, especially his own long and difficult name.

Sadia resists the temptation to pressurise Michael to write, and continues to read with him, to look at print and to offer and use 3D letters to support his knowledge of phonics, explaining her reasons to his parents and her colleagues. She offers mark-making opportunities in his preferred outdoor environment, tallying goals scored and making number plates for the bikes, and plans for den building.

One day the door is open and, unusually, Michael is not the first on the bikes. Sadia spots him busy in the block area, alone and obviously engaged. Some 10 minutes later, Michael comes to her.

'Sadia, come and see what I have done.'

There on the mat is Michael's full name, accurately laid out in blocks, using straights and curves, and with a small square block for the dot over the 'i'.

In Encounter: Michael's writing, Sadia has understood Michael's ways of learning and doing, and has the confidence to stand by her convictions. Within her enabling environment Michael has developed and demonstrated characteristics of learning that will stand him in good stead in the future: engagement, perseverance, problem-solving and creativity, to name a few. Sadia has considered his current needs, showing her concern for Michael's *being* as well as for his *becoming*.

Michael subsequently transferred to school, and learned to write successfully, though definitely later than his peers. Now grown up, he is still happy to meet Sadia and tell her the latest news of his professional career.

From consultation to participation

There has undoubtedly been progress in tuning into young children's voices and acting on what is heard but, for some, there is recognition that we can go further. If we see children as 'rich in potential, strong, powerful, competent' as Malaguzzi did, then progress will take the form of moving beyond consultation and towards participation.

When considering the role of children in research, Kellett would argue that at some levels approaches are 'tokenistic' (in Gray and Winter, 2011: 28). Discussing research with young children, he identifies that, though children are now seen as active participants in research projects, the adults continue to hold the power, by choosing the questions for research. The same can be seen in many of the case studies presented so far. The children can make choices, but within the options provided by the adults. Webster (in Moyles, 2010: 118) suggests many approaches can be used to elicit responses from children; these include photo-elicitation, drawings, puppetry, video-camera, on-line and hard copy portfolios. She cites Burke (in Thomson, 2008), who

> reminds us to be conscious of what rights we have of adults in exploring children's worlds but also to be mindful of the power relationships between adults and children. This is of particular relevance when conducting enquiry into children's lives and attempting to capture, explore and listen to children's perspectives.

Hart (1992: 8) devised a Ladder of Participation, which is widely used as a model within services for children and young people to support the promotion of their participation. Hart characterises involvement at the bottom rungs as 'non-participation' featuring 'manipulation . . . where children are consulted but given no feedback' and 'tokenism . . . in which children are apparently given a voice, but in fact have little or no choice about the subject or the style of communicating it'. In contrast, the upper rungs of the ladder denote 'levels of participation', with the top rung characterised by 'child-initiated, shared decisions with adults'. Although Hart specifically excludes preschool children from the range of his research in this instance, it is easy to see how his principles can be applied to children of that age for our purposes.

Indeed, Hart's wording is particularly useful to us, as it provides us with a means to address a possible point of contention. In 1996, Lansdown reviewed the impact and implications of the recently ratified UNCRC on children and practitioners in our context of early years. She discussed the argument current at the time, which opposed Article 12 and other related articles, namely 'Children are not competent to participate in decision making' (Lansdown, 1996: 7). She declared this to be a misconception and misunderstanding of the Article by some who understood it to advocate that children should autonomously take control of decisions, independent of adult views and responsibilities for the child. Lansdown with Lancaster (2001) was later to describe the Coram Family *Listening to Young Children Project*, which offers a model I return to often and so will include here at some length.

> Although a rights-based approach addresses traditional power relations it is not advocating young children should hold all or the majority of power. It is an approach that views young children as active and competent participants within their environment. Young children are not advanced the status of *the* expert, however – having the expertise to be the sole decision-makers in their lives. Addressing power relations is about advocating for the young child's views to be tabled along with the views of all the other active players. Inclusion to decision-making processes is not premised on the exclusion of another (parents, carers and significant others). It is rather about pulling up another chair alongside those already present.
>
> (Lansdown and Lancaster, 2001: 49)

This appears a very apt image conveying a picture of the child as contributor and participant, afforded active status from the youngest age in the decision-making process in matters that concern him.

The Early Childhood Forum (ECF) identifies five foundations of early learning. One of these is 'Contributing and Participating', and they list characteristics that include, among others, 'participating in the life of the group . . ., collaborating in shared activities . . ., contributing their unique and individual thoughts . . ., taking growing responsibility for themselves in the group . . ., learning to understand and reflect on the impact of their decisions on others' (ECF, 2003: 17). The following encounter may help to understand how this might appear in action, embodying as it does all of the characteristics listed.

The children here are being empowered to participate in recognition of their competence (Burr and Montgomery, 2003). In this setting the children are informed; they know what they are being asked to do and why. They know that their ideas may be discussed and debated with peers and adults, and that their decisions may be questioned or challenged, but that they will be acted on if they can justify them. They also know, because it has happened before, that not all of

---

ENCOUNTER: Children's priorities

The setting is a preschool that packs away its provisions at the weekend. The building is unprepossessing, a sports field changing room, but the practice is excellent. All equipment is stored in a shipping container to which the children can have no access because of issues of safety. The staff have long used their homemade 'catalogue' to enable children to request equipment that is still in the container. They have recently been watching the children rearrange the home corner furniture and have decided to hand over the decision making for this area of provision to the children. They make a new 'catalogue' of home corner and imaginative play equipment and each Friday afternoon a different pair of children in turn can choose the furniture to be brought in ready for them to arrange on Monday morning. This has some interesting results.

A pair of children arranges the furniture, then drapes it liberally with blankets and sheets, reflecting their interest in den-making outside.

One child works with his key person in an episode of sustained shared problem solving, hanging a white board from the changing room hooks to represent the shopping list on the fridge door at home. Making shopping lists is a current joint venture hugely enjoyed by child and child-minder.

Sim has just had a new baby sister. He places a cot in the middle of the room. The engaged adult discusses with him whether this is the safest and best place for the cot, which might get knocked by other children. Sim firmly states, 'They will have to know that it is important, and they will have to be careful.' To ensure that his peers do have that understanding and appreciate the importance of the cot to Sim, the practitioner arranges a group time before the other children use the home corner, in which he explains it to them.

---

their ideas will be accepted and, if not, they know that the reasons will be explained and discussed. (The plan for the Water Fight Birthday Party was adapted by negotiation to include use of the outdoors!) The children take responsibility for their decisions and can see the impact that they have. They have the choice of opting out of the consultation process, though few do. The staff have supported less confident children to participate by careful pairings, using their knowledge of the children in the group.

The immediate benefits of a culture of participation and voice

Bruner (in Rinaldi 2006) proposes an approach to learning that positions the child and educator as equal participants in an education process based on dialogue and action. Within the social constructivist perspective, learning can be seen as a social process (Vygotsky, 1933), which is embarked on by child and practitioner together, co-constructing knowledge within the shared culture and context. Listening to and closely observing children's ideas and hypotheses, particularly when a child is non-verbal or is using a first language, enables the practitioner to understand how they are making meaning of their world, allowing the adult to question, challenge, pose alternatives and develop children's understanding. In this respect, a listening culture within a setting will enable children and adults to demonstrate what they are hearing, thinking and learning. Children who see themselves as active and successful participants in their own learning are more likely to be engaged and to have a positive disposition to learning. It suggests the need for joint engagement and involvement, and implies relationships of equity and trust in learning and teaching. Although both parties must be involved in the thinking there does not necessarily need to be equal contribution to the conversation but there does need to be reciprocity in the interaction.

Brown sees such shared episodes as involving *co-construction* which she sees requires participants to work together to share and create meaning. She reiterates, 'Studying meaning requires teachers and children to make sense of the world, interpreting and understanding activities and observations as they interact with each other' (Brown, in Woods, 2015: 115).

Respecting children's existing capacities and abilities, according them equal status in learning, shifts traditional power relations, allows children to take a lead and supports their developing sense of self. Positive self-image can be gained by children who see themselves reflected in the eyes of significant others as 'rich in potential, strong, powerful, competent and, most of all, connected to adults and other children' (Malaguzzi, 1993). Active participation in the community of learners, in the life of the setting, supports a child's developing identity as a member of that particular social group with responsibility for self and others.

Practitioners who adopt a pedagogy of listening, know and understand the children in their care, and can plan and provide appropriately for them, giving due weight to their opinions and voice. This leads to more effective provision, better engaged in by the children. Staff at the setting above reported more episodes of sustained engagement in home corner play by all children when the children were in charge of its layout. Improved child involvement can improve the quality of work for the adults too, bringing, as it does, an enhanced sense of satisfaction in a job well done.

Settings that actively listen to children and encourage their participation are likely to be offering appropriate provision and experiences that involve the children to be inclusive and to be judged of high quality by the most important stake holders – the children and families.

Parents are also engaged in this virtuous circle of listening. Parents who listen get to know their children better, demonstrate respect for their children's views so can expect respect in return, and will be secure in the knowledge that their child is cared for in a setting that values their individuality.

The long-term benefits of a culture of participation and voice

Hart (1992: 4) writes:

> A nation is democratic to the extent that its citizens are involved, particularly at the community level. The confidence and competence to be involved must be gradually acquired through practice. It is for this reason that there should be gradually increasing opportunities for children to participate in any aspiring democracy, and particularly in those nations already convinced that they are democratic. With the growth of children's rights we are beginning to see an increasing recognition of children's abilities to speak for themselves.

This ideology can help us to engage in a more long-term perspective of benefits of the rights-based listening approach. Moss proposes that an early years setting, as 'a place of encounter and dialogue between citizens' (2007: 13), a 'democratic space' (Ibid.: 27), can be well suited to promote and foster democratic processes.

Early years learning within the High/Scope Perry Pre-School project is characterised by child-initiated learning and a play-based approach in which children make and are responsible for choices. Research into the effects of this model of children as active participants in their own learning provides evidence of benefits into later life in areas such as work, lawfulness, relationships and earnings (Schweinhart *et al.*, 2005). Early fostering of positive dispositions to learning may support maintenance of a positive approach in later life.

The child who learns to participate and contribute within an early years setting may be more likely to participate in society as an adult. Children who have learned that their contribution is valuable and valued are more likely to be willing to contribute to their community and society, an important aim in the future for active citizenship, fairness, justice and democracy.

The respect for others, both peers and those of a different age, and the acceptance of their individuality, which a listening culture fosters, will be increasingly valuable to children as they grow up to take their place in a diverse community within a multicultural and multi-faith world. This may result in greater social cohesion and less social exclusion.

Finally, and importantly, children who know they will be listened to respectfully and seriously are more likely to voice their concerns and ask for help, allowing them to be protected and kept safe.

Post script

The final encounter of this chapter is included by way of a warning. If a setting is trying to include children as active participants in matters that concern them, then it is important to discuss the endeavour with all those concerned.

ENCOUNTER: The party food list

Preparations for the Christmas party at the preschool have always included staff providing a list of party food for parents to volunteer to bring – all the usual things: sandwiches, jelly, crisps and chocolate fingers.

This year, however, the children draw up the list democratically, with the most popular items appearing at the top of the list. The staff are surprised to find that the top three items most popular with the children for the party are yoghurt, pizza and bananas.

The day of the party dawns and parents bring the food – all the usual things: sandwiches, jelly, crisps and chocolate fingers!

Provocations

- How do you build in time within your daily practice to tune into the voice of the children in your care? Do you share what you have heard with your colleagues so that you can act on it together?

- Can you identify a child or children whose voice you find harder to hear? What steps do you take to advocate on their behalf?

- To what extent is your setting a 'democratic space'? Can you think of a measure you could take to make it more so?

- Think of a time recently when you have enabled children's participation in decisions that are important to them. Did you share this with the children, their families, your colleagues?

References

Brown, V. (2015) Chapter 7. Sustained shared conversations. In: Woods, A. (ed.). *The Characteristics of Effective Learning. Creating and Capturing the Possibilities in the Early Years*. London: David Fulton.

Burr, R. and Montgomery, H. (2003) Children and rights. In: Woodhead, M. and Montgomery H. (eds). *Understanding Childhood: An Interdisciplinary Approach*, Chichester, UK: John Wiley in association with OUP.

Casey, T. (2010) *Inclusive Play: Practical Strategies for Children from Birth to Eight*, 2nd edn, London: Sage.

Clark, A., McQuail, S. and Moss, P. (Thomas Coram Research Unit) (2003) *Exploring the Field of Listening to and Consulting with Young Children*, Nottingham, UK: DfES.

Clark, A. and Moss, P. (2011) *Listening to Young Children: The mosaic approach*, 2nd edn, London: National Children's Bureau.

Crow, G., Foley, P. and Leverett, S. (2008) Communicating with children. In: Foley, P. and Leverett, S. (eds.). *Connecting with Children: Developing working relationships*, Bristol, UK: Policy Press in association with Open University.

Department of Education (DfE) (2012) *Statistical Release; NEET Statistics – Quarterly Brief – Quarter 1 2012*. Available online at: www.education.gov.uk/rsgateway/DB/STR/d001064/osr09-2012.pdf (accessed 1 August 2012).

Department for Education and Skills (DfES) (2003) Every Child Matters: Presented to Parliament by the Chief Secretary to the Treasury by Command of Her Majesty, September 2003, Cm 5860, London: Stationery Office.

Early Childhood Forum (ECF) (2003) *Quality in Diversity in Early Learning: A framework for early childhood practitioners*, London: National Children's Bureau.

Edwards, S., Cutter-Mackenzie, A. and Hunt, E. (2010) Chapter 10. Framing play for learning. Professional reflections on the role of open-ended play in early childhood education. In: Brooker, L. and Edwards, S. (eds.). *Engaging Play*. Maidenhead, UK: OUP.

Gray, C. and Winter, E. (2011) The ethics of participatory research involving young children with special needs. In: Harcourt, D., Perry, B. and Waller, T. (eds.). *Researching Young Children's Perspectives: Debating the ethics and dilemmas of educational research with children*, London: Routledge.

Hart, R. A. (1992) *Children's Participation: From tokenism to citizenship*, Florence: UNICEF.

Laming, Lord (2003) *The Victoria Climbie Inquiry: Report of an inquiry by Lord Laming*. London: The Stationery Office. Available online at: www.dh.gov.uk/prod_consum_dh/groups/dh_digitalassets/documents/digitalasset/dh_110711.pdf (accessed 15 May 2011).

Lancaster, Y. P. and Broadbent, V. (2003) *Listening to Young Children*, Maidenhead, UK: OUP.

Lancaster, Y. P. and Kirby, P. (2010) *Listening to Young Children*, 2nd edn, Maidenhead, UK: OUP.

Lane, J. (2008) *Young Children and Racial Justice: Taking action for racial equality in the early years – understanding the past, thinking about the present, planning for the future*, London: National Children's Bureau.

Lansdown, G. (1996) The United Nations convention on the Rights of the Child – Progress in the United Kingdom. In: Nutbrown, C. (ed.). *Respectful Educators – Capable Learners: Children's rights and early education*, London: Paul Chapman.

Lansdown, G. and Lancaster, Y. P. (2001) Promoting children's welfare by respecting their rights. In: Pugh, G. (ed.). *Contemporary Issues in the Early Years, Working Collaboratively for Children*, 3rd edn, London: Paul Chapman.

Löfdahl, A. (2010) Chapter 9. Peer groups, power and play in early childhood settings. In Brooker, L. and Edwards, S. (eds.). *Engaging Play*. Maidenhead, UK: OUP.

Malaguzzi, L. (1993) For an education based on relationships, *Young Children*, 11(93): 9–13.

Moran, M. (2006) Getting to know you, *Nursery World*, 31 September 2006. Available online at: www.nurseryworld.co.uk/news/711894/Getting-know/?DCMP=ILC-SEARCH (accessed 14 May 2012).

Mortimer, H. with SureStart Stockton-on-Tees (2007) *Listening to Children in their Early Years*, Lichfield, UK: QEd.

Moss, P. (2007) *Bringing Politics into the Nursery: Early childhood education as a democratic practice*. Working Paper 43. The Hague, The Netherlands: Bernard van Leer Foundation.

Moss, P. and Petrie, P. (2002) *From Children's Services to Children's Spaces: Public policy, children and childhood*, London: RoutledgeFalmer.

Rinaldi, C. (2006) *In Dialogue with Reggio Emilia: Listening, researching and learning*, Abingdon, UK: Routledge.

Ryan, S. (2005) Freedom to choose: Examining children's experiences in choice time. In: Yelland, N. (ed.). *Critical Issues in Early Childhood Education*, Maidenhed, UK: OUP.

Schweinhart, L. J., Montie, J., Xiang, Z., Barnett, W. S., Belfield, C. R. and Nores, M. (2005) *Lifetime Effects: The HighScope Perry Preschool study through age 40*. (Monographs of the HighScope Educational Research Foundation, 14.) Ypsilanti, MI: HighScope Press.

Smidt, S. (2013) *The Developing Child in the 21st Century. A Global Perspective on Child Development*, 2nd edn. London: Routledge.

The Children Act (2004) (c.145) London: HMSO.

United Nations (UN) (1989) *Convention on the Rights of the Child*, New York: United Nations.

Vygotsky, L. S. (1933) Play and its role in the mental development of the child, *Soviet Psychology*. Available online at: www.marxists.org/archive/vygotsky/works/1933/play.htm (accessed 17 August 2011).

Webster, R. (2010) Chapter 7. Listening to and learning from children's perspectives. In Moyles, J. (ed.). *Thinking About Play. Developing a Reflective Approach*. Maidenhead, UK: OUP.

Exploiting outdoor possibilities for all children

Annie Woods and Val Hall

The outdoors stimulates and excites children of all ages enabling them to explore and discover fascinating worlds and experience offerings richly provided in the natural world; as Edwards states: 'Everyone knows that children would rather be out than in. . . . There are more vivid, more practical, more inspiring ways of finding out about the world we live in' (2002, cited in Day, 2007: 177). Providing possibilities for play both indoors and out are vital. Wilson (2012: 92) cites E. O. Wilson'stheory of biophilia, which claims 'people are biologically attracted to nature and need frequent contact with it to find fulfilment (Kellert and Wilson, 1993; Quinn, 1996). If some children's access to nature is limited, their chances of finding fulfilment through the natural world are also limited'. Reasons are rarely given why children are not able to play indoors, but how many times might you have heard, or said, *'too hot' 'too cold' 'too wet' 'too dangerous'* all with children's best interest in mind with regards to playing outdoors? Our intention within this chapter is not to provide you with a manual or a handbook of activities for children outdoors but, through a series of encounters, a meander on a journey exploring outdoor possibilities for all children. Adults who support and sustain the world outdoors acknowledge the benefits it provides, yet the advantages and individual qualities the outdoors present are often the very same characteristics that challenge adults; for example, temperature, wetness, wildness, space, insects and open boundaries, which children appear to seek and manage themselves. We would suggest that children's playfulness also appears to challenge an adult's desire to control the learning environment *for* children. Carefree feelings and the spirit of childhood may often diminish as we grow older, replaced instead by responsibilities and a need to be aware of pitfalls and dangers to those we perceive as more susceptible to risk; it is these perceptions that are challenged in Chapter 5, and ones we will gently begin to tease out here.

Parents and practitioners frequently want to exploit the potential of the outdoors and yet our own prejudices, fears, concerns or lack of specialist skills may hinder us achieving the best learning experiences for our children. We have to accept that not all adults enjoy the outdoors and this may be linked to personal childhood experiences or developed in recent years as the need for comfort and dry clothing takes priority over battling wet and windy weather. We are asking for you to try to look again through a child's eyes as to the opportunities you might offer them by giving them possible links with the outdoors; dress yourselves *and* the children appropriately.

Inclusive play

Consider then if our children face additional obstacles or have complex needs and the task becomes greater still. Planning for possibilities, by considering how to overcome real and perceived barriers, asks you to recall, not in a purely nostalgic sense, what it is like to be a child outdoors, but be responsible for promoting positive adult attitudes towards outdoor play while working alongside confident peers, enabling you to create a culture of inclusivity.

This first encounter demonstrates a risk staff had perceived and the sensible, easy precautions to counter it. During the preschool woodland experiences children have occasionally stung themselves; we have not removed the nettles as the ladybirds like them. The children have rarely cried and we encourage them not to scratch the rash, but to find a dock leaf to wrap the hand/leg/finger in. The children gain the idea that minor hurts can be dealt with and they have identified two plants.

ENCOUNTER: Exploring the woodland before the first forest school session

There are stinging nettles. We have agreed four rules: children are to not eat anything or pick any living materials, and they are not to squash living creatures and must keep within the boundaries. These will be explained at the gate when parents have dropped them off.

On the first visit, we will walk the children on the left hand side, where there is a clear path and views to the fields. At the bottom of the wood is a large cleared space with some trees for beginner climbers – one branch, and space to identify a 'home tree' for returning to. There are also four trees that can act as shelter poles for a tarpaulin. It has a natural boundary within the woodland.

We discussed initial walking, interests for children to emerge, photographing the wood, hide and seek in groups and general exploration as key to the first two visits. We talked further of digging, potions, role-play cooking, dream catchers, clay on trunks, tying sticks together. It was agreed that children's interests should emerge as leading our practice.

There are still concerns with preschool practitioners with regards to risk; it is a real step into the unknown to not provide indoor equipment such as clip boards, and there are worries about getting cold, hurt, wet or lost.

The encounter also shows how the inexperienced practitioners perceived the need and the security of 'known' equipment to give to the children. In the weeks we have used the woodlands, any of the few resources we have taken in the rucksack have been used only in response to a deep level of activity . . . a magnifying glass, a trowel, a clipboard for recording the number of ladybirds and a torch for the tree-based tent created by two boys. The staff, gradually letting go and absorbing themselves in the child-led, playful explorations, have emerged as quieter, more reflective and more natural co-constructors of new experiential understanding.

The outdoor environment provides opportunities for all children of any age and gender, including some of our most vulnerable and challenging children, to reach their full potential. A philosophy of inclusive outdoor play enables us to incorporate principles of imagination, creativity and positive risk taking. A vision of outdoor play for all children encourages us to exploit possibilities and celebrate personal achievements, and as Hart *et al.* (2004: 4) remind us 'Learning without limits becomes possible when young children's school experiences are not organized and structured on the basis of judgements of ability'.

Legislation ensures the protection of children's rights and the promotion of inclusive play (UNCRC, 1989; Education Act, 1996; Disability Discrimination Act, 2005; Discrimination Act, 2010) safeguarding children to protect and promote inclusive play so that no child is disadvantaged or excluded. This chapter considers that practitioners and parents should work together and embrace inclusive outdoor play and as a result embed these principles within their practice. If all adults were to hold these fundamental beliefs, the necessity for laws to enforce the rights of children to play would be redundant. Instead parents and practitioners are able to take ownership of the outdoors and transmit their positivity to their children, rather than a reluctance to 'get stuck in'. Knowledgeable adults do not need legislation to inform or convince them of the benefits of the outdoors for their children, however, legislation does protect and strengthen the foundations of this play. 'Inclusive practice offers the opportunity to explore our assumptions, open up our processes and ways of working so as to build bridges between experiences' (Nind *et al.*, 2005: 138).

What we must be mindful of, however, is hiding behind our interpretations of legislation and non-statutory guidance as an excuse for not exploiting the outside. Convincing us that outdoor play is too hazardous and requires too much form filling and paperwork to be beneficial is not the purpose of legislation.

Natural resources

Outdoor play environments are rich in nature's sensory gifts, helping to stimulate children and encourage them to confront and engage with everyday experiences, developing choices and emotional resilience. We would further suggest that the natural elements *only* experienced outside seem to instinctively draw children to enjoy themselves, refining their sensory, creative, imaginary, linguistic and, of course, physical skills. We are unable to provide large-scale water/rain, the wind in the trees with scudding clouds, glorious, oozing and squelchy mud and the excitement of fire indoors.

Helping to light and sustain a fire, running in and out of puddles is joyful and we must remember our youngest children and their sensory opportunities outside. Babies and toddlers enjoy the feel of grass and sand and mud, watching the trees move and catching their breath in the stiff breeze. Playing outdoors clearly is not just for independently mobile children and many settings are organising for sleep sessions outdoors as well as periods of time experiencing the weather, wind chimes, reflective hanging objects, ribbons waving, drifting gauze-like materials and the rain pattering on umbrellas and silver foil. Try creating a den from hypothermia blankets when the tinkle of rain drops gently on the top and watch carefully the resulting delight.

Let us not underestimate the nervousness of colleagues, inexperienced themselves in outdoor learning and adventure. Undertaking training, using supportive others, apprenticeship with confident practitioners *should* help overcome some of the perceived difficulties we see in those unwilling to use the outdoor environment. Adults, too, must be seen as unique; they too need an enabling environment given positive reinforcement by others and opportunities to learn and develop. This will mean parents being able to access and enjoy outdoor sites, too.

Play outdoors should be significantly different from both indoor play with natural materials, and outdoor provision where the indoor curriculum is merely replicated in gestures or labelled learning areas. This tokenistic approach suggests that practitioners are looking to 'capture' children who prefer to be outdoors, and engage them in '*what they feel they should be doing*'. We all might recall planning for those children who want to use all the boundaries of our outdoor space, on foot or on wheels, a writing station in a role play garage . . . rarely is the writing activity sustained or meaningful when it is the space, the speed, the distance, the

---

ENCOUNTER: The possibility of puddles . . .

Phone call from practitioners. Having visited the woodland, they have rung to cancel the session this week as they feel the puddles are too deep and the children might drown. They sent a picture taken on a camera phone. The puddles, for me, look quite exciting and full of possibilities. We have branches for potential bridge-making; the children have already played out games with fishing rods on dry earth. I am unable to accompany them this week and the practitioners feel vulnerable. The week after, the puddles were deeper, but with my support, we had the most glorious play. The following week, I mentioned that I had seen a fire pit that I thought would be perfect for the setting. Jane's response was that she would 'leave that to me' as she was not ready for fire.

self-challenge, the air in the face, the game engendered between a social group that engages children. Engaged children will find the whole learning environment stimulating and we suggest they are more likely to put together a record of photographs, captions and labels when they are ready. Finding a rabbit hole and the pile of rabbit droppings outside it, a small group of children then rushed back to the rucksack, emptied and ransacked it, to find the laminated sheets to 'mark-up' their find. This is meaningful writing engagement. When considering the possibilities of planning from *those* interests, we are reminded of Broadhead and Burt's (2012: 26) reflection:

> We were finding that the outdoor area was being led by the children's interests whereas the indoors was still being driven by topic-related planning. The topic based approach required a deal of planning time and the curricular repetition seemed increasingly less interesting for staff so it became harder to think about enthusing the children.

Planning for possibilities is taking a pair of secateurs to the wood and waiting for what the children have been observed to be ready to use, rather than deliberately preparing to teach the skill.

ENCOUNTER: The language of ladybirds

Freddie (with ladybird): He loves me. He wants to come home with me. (Voicing for ladybird) I can't fly as I have no wings. I can only be his pet. (To me) Why can ladybirds swap legs when they walk? Long way to climb up, maybe he can climb all the way up here. Wait and see. He can climb up my zip. He's never gonna fly off me. He can climb up the tree (lifts onto tree).

The thing that strikes me is the level and time the children take to talk. It might start with narrating their current activity or interest . . . counting ladybirds, for example, but the outdoors affords them the time and space and attentive adult or peer to range far and wide in their talk.

One child recalled that his favourite thing today was talking to Linda (adult).

Jane (adult) told me how surprised and pleased she was that Freddie had talked to me for so long as 'he would not do that at preschool'.

Freddie voiced what he liked today. (First time he has used recall time at the end of the session.)

Descriptive language very evident today as insects appeared to focus their attention. Much more engaging than introducing a topic on minibeasts.

I will plan to take secateurs next week and anticipate the possibility that Freddie will want to create a house for the ladybirds; my aim is not to take him aside to teach him, but to be ready should the opportunity arise.

The adult, attuned to the child, will *expect* they will be useful to the child because of an enduring and developing interest in scaling down twigs; the planning is the 'what might happen, and as an adult have I anticipated and resourced this', rather than 'all children will be taught how to use secateurs'.

Playing outdoors

The distinctive nature of the outdoors enables children to experiment and play in ways that are all their own. White (2008: 7) reminds us that, 'outdoor provision is an essential part of the child's daily environment and life, not an option or an extra.' The outdoor environment enables children to have experiences indoor environments find difficult to replicate, for example, large-scale uneven terrain, natural sensory materials and unpredictable weather conditions. Outdoor features contribute to the quality of the child's learning and, done well, the amount of fun experienced. Here we need to consider access, inclusion and participation (Wilson, 2012) for all children. 'Can a child be included in an activity? Do they feel part of a group? Can they sit together, fit at the table, find a space in the den?' (Ibid.: 120). Children's connections with the outdoors and the natural world are more than merely dispositions to educate; they provide a necessary link to the cycle of inter-dependence. Play outdoors may provide safe-havens, exhilaration or even provoke fear. Extremes of emotions challenge and stimulate, sparking sensations children may not otherwise encounter. Embracing or even conquering each experience provides moments for children to celebrate and take pride in their achievements.

Extremes of reactions are all possible when confronting and engaging in play in the outdoors. As Day (2007:180) suggests,

> it's hard to study much that is alive – only a few things can live indoors, and only when separated from their living context. Context gives meaning to things. Separation isolates them – from life, from relationships, from time continuum, and in our thinking. Not a good way to learn about the environment – which is all about life, relationships, time, linkage and wholeness.

What is noticeable is the sustained talk that takes place in the natural environment, particularly when the terrain is without artificial or added fixed features. Children

ENCOUNTER: Trees

Every week at recall time, one of the children will say 'climbing trees, climbing higher than Jane'; 'swinging up in the tree upside down'.

ENCOUNTER: Counting ladybirds

Jonah: Look, there's another ladybird. 1, 2, 3, 4. If we find another one, that will make 5. Jonah to Ned: Shall we work as a team and go and find ladybirds? Let's go find some more. Ned: (singing) We are going to dig, dig, dig, dig. That makes 7 after 6.

---

who rarely interact or talk with other children appear to 'work and play above themselves', engaging with natural mathematics and physics, which as adults we need to note, engage with and plan for, using their outdoor interests to guide the indoor curriculum and not vice versa. The Encounter: Counting ladybirds was part of an extended interest in ladybirds that morning, who emerging into the sunlight to shake their wings, became a natural source for counting, and counting on, as well as a stimulus for a deep level care.

Linda and Jane, discussing creativity outdoors, initially found it difficult to move beyond '*taking the inside out*'. During discussions the idea of supplementing what was already available outdoors, as in Encounter: The language of ladybirds, became a real possibility. In one of the final sessions outside, a different practitioner came to the woods to play for the first time, and I was interested to see paintbrushes, magnifying glasses and other tools placed in 'fan like' groups as we might find them on classroom tables.

Play for children often relies on friendships and a sense of acceptance. Play enables children to build friendships and gain understanding of their own individual needs. A non-judgmental atmosphere may support children through uncertainties as they develop their friendships and progress on their journey of acceptance. Ludvigsen *et al.* (2005: 3) state 'At its best inclusion enables all children – of all abilities, ethnic backgrounds, ages and other differences – to play together'.

Well-planned activities outdoors may have no right answer or outcome and should challenge children at their own level, and it may be that as adults we are apprehensive of the powerful, experiential outcomes that children set and meet themselves. Child-initiated activity, hypotheses and questions *should* excite, challenge and afford us the opportunity for research and learning. Banning and Sullivan (2011: 8) argue that

> Children in rich outdoor environments can stay busy all day long with little or no prompting from adults. Give ample time to explore and rich materials to discover, children and their outdoor environment function as a unit – inseparable and connected.

Perceived barriers and challenges

Casey (2007: 12) points out that, 'a culture of participation is important to the development of inclusive play'. The key to inclusive play in the outdoors is the pedagogical approach adopted and the quality of the affordance of the experience itself, for all children.

> Since all children are unique and their play takes many forms and directions, the wider the variety of play and ways of playing the environment supports the more inclusive it is of children with a wide range of abilities and needs.
>
> (Ibid.: 35)

Play provides realistic opportunities for all children to develop their characters. Remember back to your own childhood experiences considering moments of daring, heightened enthusiasm and passionate responses; eager participants willing to test themselves and encounter fear/exhilaration head on. Play, particularly in the outdoors, is a fundamental part of childhood. Gargiulo and Kilgo (2011: 243) argue that 'Play is the work of the child and a natural mechanism for facilitating inclusive experiences.' Children actively engage in play developing individual qualities and skills and further,

> if early years environments limit the possibilities for pursuing personal interests, memories and experiences, they are potentially also limiting the possibilities for strong identity formation and the growth of resilience through playful engagements with peers and adults.
>
> (Broadhead and Burt, 2012: 48)

Inclusive play offers children choices yet at times there may be barriers restricting those choices. The first steps to breaking down barriers involve recognition and understanding of the essential elements contributing to the barrier. We need to acknowledge that as potential and reluctant practitioners outside engaging with children absorbed in *their* playful interests, we may find excuses not to do so . . . too cold, too hot, too dirty, too wet, too time consuming to get them all water-proofed. . . . It may of course be that their play is beyond our understanding and they may be unwilling for us to join in, and it is worthy of future research to try to tease out why some children develop into reluctant outdoor adults.

Many do not, and we appear to be currently experiencing a resurgence in providing opportunities for outdoor play; for example in the Bristol street play project, forest schools and 'nomadic' outdoor forest sessions across London. We suggest that there are always opportunities to demonstrate our willingness, ability and readiness to recognise when they want us to be playful, understanding, and supportive to follow their lead. Henricks (2010, cited in Broadhead and Burt, 2012: 19) argues that adults routinely judge children to be 'at play' because they see no consequences for the activity beyond the event itself. They add, in the perceived absence of 'outcome' the play activity is often deemed low status . . . and outdoor play, we suggest, can appear to be both more playful and perceived as having recreational value only. We have a duty to continually articulate the value of child-led, outdoor deep-level learning about the world, the self and others as children test out theories and experience a sense of wonder at their smallest find or discovery. We also need appropriate clothes ourselves: waterproofs, boots, fleeces, hats and gloves, ready for action, ready to work and play.

We need to consider designing inclusive-friendly spaces. A summary of suggestions from Wilson (2012) and Jeavons (in Elliott, 2008) is included below; here, we also have to consider access to our outdoor space on site or a short journey away for all children, staff and parents. Every day, loose object play has to be stored or left safely in an enclosed playground, for example. Resources and equipment may need to be carried. For more adventurous outdoor play, access for all staff, parents and children needs to be straightforward; parents and staff with disability, and parents with pushchairs will want to be included, too.

When developing participation for all children, modification to environments to promote accessibility may be a starting point. Parents of children who require high levels of support appear most dissatisfied with access to organised outdoor play provision (Mills and Gleave, 2010). Parents comment that play spaces may be unsuitable for their child's special needs. There are times when it is necessary to make alterations to be able to develop successful inclusive play outdoors. Gargiulo and Kilgo (2011: 229) stress the importance of 'accessibility and safety' as 'two of the primary concerns'. Managing adjustments to the environment may be delicate as specialist equipment and accessible-friendly spaces may isolate children and parents with disabilities further. Language is also important, what we call something may dictate what we do with it. Consider 'disabled toilets' and think then in terms of 'accessible toileting'. The terminology influences our perception, the first suggests that the space is *only* for those with a disability, the second that this is a space accessible to all and provides suitable access to those with a disability. It is essential that 'adaptations should be subtle and unobtrusive as possible to minimize pointing out the differences' (Gargiulo and Kilgo, 2011: 234). Increasing access to sensory play is something children with additional needs say themselves they would like (Mills and Gleave, 2010). Sloping, winding paths, going up and down instead of steps, through low level, highly scented and different textured plants is intriguing for all, especially if a number of bends obscure a sculpture, or some rocks or reflections on water. . . .

Wilson (2003: 244) points out that 'knowing the nature of a child's disability suggests the appropriateness of certain adaptations.' Providing unique environments may not always be a realistic possibility to overcome barriers, however, considering idiosyncratic solutions through creative thinking may be. The social model of disability postulates that 'disabled people are only "disabled" because society obstructs them in some way' (Davy and Gallagher, 2006: 144). Providing opportunities to participate fully within the outdoors reduces or eliminates exclusion.

Table 4.1 Summary of suggestions for creating inclusive spaces from Jeavons

Seamless physical access into natural playspace; path systems.	Gently graded, firm and even surface; some deliberate textures and bumps for experience of sensations; wheel stops, rails, hand supports. Hierarchy of paths– smaller paths for sense of space leading to tiny areas, circuits, raised and textured edges or contrasting coloured edges.
Front-on accessibility for wheelchairs and pushchairs.	Knee room underneath tables and activities; adjustable tables, raised troughs, open sides to equipment.
Seating for carers and disabled carers.	Perching places, seats.
Calming, accessible space for those children who are frustrated and/or upset.	Small size scale away from fast routes and thoroughfare, partially enclosed with places to sit, lie, gaze, dream or rest.
Natural dens and small spaces.	Weeping type shrubs in circle/half-circle; wide opening; wheelable surface; improvised furniture with moveable logs and branches; fabric drapes; link to sand/digging area; wheelchair trays; wide tree tunnel; hammocks.
Sand	Sloping, beached edge; leaning wedge, raised sand table; relocatable mats to allow wheeling into sand.
Water	Moveable troughs, water wall accessible for standing or wheelchairs; multi-level sand and water area; adapted taps and fixings for all children to use, including foot pedals.
Gardening	Raised beds, strawberry pots, hanging baskets, teepees and arbors with vertical scented and vegetable plants for tasting; hay bales for sitting/leaning/growing; potato sacks or tyre stacks.
Animals	Small domestic rabbits, guinea pigs, fish tanks, raised pond, bird tables and bird baths.
Loose parts	Natural range with addition of torches, head torches, large magnifying glasses, binoculars.
Equipment	Straps on swings, bucket seats; fold-up ramps; embed slide in side of hill.

Source: Elliot, 2008:108–131

Boys and girls go out to play

Tucker and Matthews look at gendered-spaces giving an off-limit message. Pellegrini (2005) shows the physicality of boys compared to girls on school playgrounds. Garrick (2009) also provides a captivating window on gender play differences demonstrating how outdoor play provides opportunities for children to develop personality and identity.

A typical encounter in early years settings demonstrates how gender might impact early on children's outdoor play. It is not unusual to find girls playing with toys and equipment outside in singular ways, preferring to stay within boundaries set up by practitioners, while boys typically seek competitive, physical pursuits

---

ENCOUNTER: Using spaces

Watching young children in an early years setting playing outside I saw girls carefully building sand castles in the sand tray, decorating them with shells and flower petals picked from the nearby garden. Other girls played with farm animals on the grass, constructing tiny habitats. Boys yelping and screeching rampaged around. They dodged in and out skilfully manoeuvring around other children and equipment, enjoying games of tag and chase. Other boys rolling tyres in a competition to see who could run fast and catch the tyre before it wobbled and fell to the floor.

---

travelling outside of organised areas of play. Boys appear to 'modify the landscape' as opposed to the imaginative movement of girls; 'bushes became walls, branches became shelves' (Hart, 1978, cited in Bilton, 2010: 158). We need to acknowledge our own perceptions and expectations here; as in our observations, the more natural the environment, the less stereotypical play is observed.

Lindon (2001: 92) explores outdoor language, and finds that girls prefer to 'talk more'. Engaging in alternative play may help to develop language. Earlier, Freddie (in an earlier encounter) was seen to self–narrate and talk to adults who are sitting close by; this was not what the practitioners had expected to see or listen to. A longer encounter also shows how intimate social and imaginative play challenges our expectations of the physical nature of young boys' play.

ENCOUNTER: 'Rats'

Small woodland animals had been left in the tent for children to discover and decide how they wanted to play with them during the forest school session. A small group of boys [Archie, Sonny and Seb] had taken them to the base of a tree, which had a hole at ground level and a mossy mound.

Archie: All the rats will eat him up. They don't live there, they go under; they eat in here. They live under. Do you see this one?

[All boys hold small animals]

That's stopped rats getting them. Yeah, you see? I stopped the rats getting them. Stop the rats! The rats will eat the mud up.

Sonny: The rats will eat the mud up. I got a lady here. Where's my little hole?

Seb: I'm making the hole there.

[Thomas comes to take photo of hole]

Sonny: I can make holes. Pow, pow, pow, pow, pow, pow.

Archie: What are you trying to play?

Seb: Now go down my hole. It will be dangerous.

Sonny: It can Seb.

Archie: Are you scary? I'm scary. I scare rats when they come out at night time. They can't scare me either.

Sonny: I will be in my hole. See, it's dangerous. There's a bigger hole. Don't get in there, it's dangerous (to Sonny). No, don't – making it wider. No-one allowed to go in, only squirrels.

[Thomas keeps taking photos]

Sonny: Make it even wider.

Archie: I made a big hole. Aah.

Seb: Wow! That's very massive. We're making a bigger one than you. We only need friends, we are brothers. [Sonny and Seb are twin brothers].

Archie: I like big holes though, Sonny. There are no chickens in this hole, only nuts. [using different voice-: I like nuts. Seb, there are blue nuts. I like pink nuts. I'm struggling in bed.] Look at my big hole. It's even bigger than yours.

[Sonny and Seb are scooping, gouging, digging]

Archie: I like pink nuts. You like pink nuts? I only like pink nuts and blue nuts.

Seb: Let's go

Sonny: It's very deep.

Archie: No-one come in now, you can come in.

Sonny: There's a very deep hole.

Archie: What are you holding?

Seb: Hedgehog. And we're not letting him in there.

Archie: [new voice] Hello. I'm a fox. I'm not a fox anymore, I've turned into something else. Can I (the hedgehog) dig? He's got paws.

Seb: You not allowed.

Archie: Am I allowed to go in?

Seb: Not allowed under the tunnel, you will get stuck.

Archie: We're making holes, James. Where's the fox?

Sonny: The rabbit is down the hole.

Archie: How did he get in?

Thirty minutes play. The adult leader remarks that she rarely saw such sustained play at preschool, heads together, narrating story.

ENCOUNTER: Recall

Alice recalls: 'I just playing with Andrew in puddle and getting hands wet and climbing trees.'

Woods (2016b: 82):

> Crossing gender behavioural norms in early childhood may be difficult for children. Kane (2006) argues that boys often find this the most difficult as they are often subjected to the most ridicule. Guiding children's play or attempts to steer them in specific directions may be convincing strategies. Tackling the root cause of gender differences, and it may be in our own perceptions, and discovering where they originate are not straightforward, neither are they often within the competences of practitioners in everyday relationships with children. Better still to recognise gender differences and use this as a starting point as well as challenge the idea that boys are *naturally* kinaesthetic, when we would argue that all playful learning is active.

Gender-neutral spaces work best with supportive terminology. Yelland (2003: 154) discusses how 'gender-tagged' areas reinforce 'gender-stereotyped' messages. It is important that adults recognise their use of language in the promotion of inclusive play; this includes the use of verbal praise. Rewarding children verbally helps to create a positive atmosphere of play in the outdoors, helping children to develop accepted views of what is possible. 'Boys will be boys' linked to boisterous play suggests 'girls will be girls' in different, less physical pursuits. Parents have a direct role to play in supporting gender-friendly play, not only in the attitudes they transmit but also in practical terms considering the toys, equipment and range of activities they provide and the clothing they dress their children in to enable outdoor play. Girls in dresses may feel uncomfortable about climbing trees or being involved in rough and tumble play; better still to consider robust, flexible clothing allowing movement and the possibility of messy adventures the same as their boy counterparts. You need to be able to talk easily about this to parents.

Diverse needs

Ethnicity has also been shown to impact on outdoor play with geographic clusters of ethnicity linked to a reduction in access to green space (CABE, 2010). Use of space also varies with those from black and ethnic minority groups typically using the outdoors for 'social bonding' rather than 'exercise' (CABE, 2010: 14). This may have an impact on children's willingness to enjoy the outside environment fully.

Medical needs may also inhibit children accessing the outdoors to its fullest. Protecting children against realistic worries to safeguard their health is sensible. It would be foolhardy to expose children to extremes of temperature, high pollen counts or to ignore the status of their health each day. Sensible precautions and medical training for adults are essential in responding to specific issues. Regardless, each case should be individually and continually assessed to ensure children have the fullest access possible for them. Rethinking how we provide basic care by embracing the outdoors provides us with interesting solutions. When considering shade to protect a child from the elements, instead of artificial canopies, better still a forest canopy or sheltering under a den's tarpaulin. Dipping toes in a stream to cool down or fanning yourself with leaves provides natural alternatives and enjoyable experiences. The experiences have to be psychologically safe as well as accessible, inclusive and participative. Casey (2010: 30) suggests that we include areas to deal with stress, sensory overload, needing time away from other children, wanting to be in the vicinity of other children but not closely engaged with them, or a very real need to use their body in a more expansive way. Physical, social and emotional dispositions all contribute to the child's view of the world. Additional impairments may also impact on this world-view. Children's abilities and desires to play should not be underestimated, or their ability to make choices regarding the range of activities they wish to enjoy or their willingness to consider and manage risk.

Indoors and outdoors

Outdoor inclusive spaces are particularly important for children with special needs as the outdoors may 'offer unique opportunities that may not be replicated indoors' (Kein *et al.*, 2001: 74). For any child the outdoors may be considered challenging or even risky. Adults often bring their own experiences to bear when assessing risk for the children in their care. Abandoning considerations of risk in developing inclusive outdoor play would be foolish, but adopting a gradual approach to risk management enables adults to develop experience and confidence, their self-assurance then translating into realistic support for their children.

Considerations of risk for children with special needs may cloud the issue of risk. 'Disabled children are sometimes over-protected and needlessly kept inside' (Ouvry, 2005: 21). Protecting vulnerable children against possible hazards they may encounter in the outdoors is a realistic concern of parents and practitioners. Lindon (2011: 50–1) draws attention to judgments of 'acceptable risk' and highlights that 'disabled children need to have the normal tumbles of childhood'.

Realistic approaches to risk, particularly for our most vulnerable children, improve with our understanding; 'Knowledge is power' (Knight, 2011: 115) when enabling adults to increase their confidence and readiness to extend the range of activities provided for children and be alert to possibilities. Even extreme adventures outdoors, such as wheelchair abseiling, zip wires and canoeing, all then become realistic possibilities.

Adults have an important role in enabling children access to outdoor play; this is magnified for children with special needs. In cases where children's impairments reduce their ability to access the outdoors independently, adult intervention is critical. Garrick (2009: 64) points to adults needing to be 'proactive' in promoting inclusive outdoor play. Children with additional needs frequently require adults to be an enabler. Creating harmony between adult support and respect for children's independence is key to building relationships. Dickens and Denziloe (2003: 14) express the need for adults to balance the degree of 'adult intervention' and the knowledge of when to 'be ready to withdraw'. Knowing children well helps us to be led by them, the adventure is then a joint one, for them knowing how much they might be able to do and for us knowing how much we are able to let them. This approach very much reflects the practice in Reggio Emilia where a co-constructive ethos underpins pedagogical practice.

Children appear more able to play and learn independently and imaginatively outdoors, perhaps needing adults less and thus creating a vacuum where adults either feel the need to interfere or subvert play. The adults' own agenda, if not carefully managed, may conflict with the freedom and desires the child seeks. This has been explored in Chapter 3. Adults faced with curriculum demands or protective issues may exert too much power in the teacher–learner relationship. For children who need autonomy in the outdoors, their play may be de-stabilised when restrictions are placed upon them. Adults may not have a sense of knowing how to play and interact with children who competently demonstrate their own learning journey and interests, and that might be laying under a tree gazing, smelling, watching, listening for what may seem like hours. For adults who are particularly responsible for individual children, this different relationship can present uncertainty: '*how and when do I join in?*' The typical relationship between an adult carer and a child with

---

ENCOUNTER: Perspectives on play

I remember the response of a parent when she saw bruises on her child's knees. David had profound and multiple learning difficulties and we had ingeniously rigged a device he could propel by kicking his legs when laid over it. Even though we had strapped knee and elbow pads to him we had not considered the softness of his skin, unused to physical exertion of this kind. As staff we had been very nervous of mum's response. Her reaction was enlightening, 'don't worry, these are the football bruises he will never have!'

ENCOUNTER: Abseiling

It was terrifying for me to see James strapped into his wheelchair, descending over the top of the cliff. Heights have always been a problem for me and even the sight of secured ropes and trained climbers either side did little to reassure me. The smile and giggles from James did! The framed photo my enthusiastic colleague (the organiser of the event) gave me is a treasured reminder serving to demonstrate that my role is to support opportunities in the outdoors, however extreme, challenging or daunting.

special needs requires new levels of trust. Adults need to readjust their convictions regarding children's levels of independence and have faith in the child's abilities to cope with new surroundings. It is not always a necessity to rush and meet each new challenge head on. Gradual phases of independence may be the most supportive and gentle means for both adult and child.

There are those children who are reluctant to venture into the outdoors. Previous encounters with children on the autistic spectrum in particular evidence children's extreme reactions to the outdoors. The changeable nature of the outdoors frequently invites children and yet, like Miles in the Encounter: Sometimes you do . . . sometimes you don't, there are those who are, at times, unwilling to accept this invitation. 'For some young children, outdoor time represents the most isolating and intimidating time of the day . . . they remain on the sidelines, observing but not fully participating' (Wilson, 2008: 79). Acknowledging the needs of this group of children may be troubling to practitioners who attempt to coax children to experience something that ultimately they might enjoy and that their initial reluctance may prevent them from connecting with. Bringing the outdoors in will surely help here. How exciting to have logs, trunks and branches, tarpaulins for sand, gravel and bark, calm and den-like spaces indoors rather than large, primary coloured, plastic soft play! When venturing out consider enticing children by hiding favourite toys in branches and undergrowth and along narrow, smaller paths to calm spaces; skills can easily be practised in simple hide and seek games indoors. Supporting such children may be simply to recognise their need and provide safe havens.

Everyday outdoor play requires practitioners to have an understanding and shared philosophy regarding the nature of play. Playtimes are typically seen to be *free-play*. We need clarity where children who have limited play skills or a reluctance to play might be encouraged. This should not conflict with the child's rights *not to play* but we need to acknowledge a difference between *not wanting* to and *not yet able to*. DeKlyen and Odom (1989, cited in Nabors *et al.*, 2001: 183) show that 'teacher-mediated play' is supportive and often involves strategies and interventions, for instance buddy systems, adult and peer modelling and the expansion of familiar games and activities to the unfamiliar. All are designed to promote inclusive play.

ENCOUNTER: Sometimes you do . . . sometimes you don't

Outdoor play for Miles was unpredictable. At difficult times of day he could be observed refusing to put on his coat, removing his shoes and telling his teachers 'No!' Any amount of cajoling would not result in him venturing outside. Later the same day Miles might be found eager to play out, so keen he would abandon his shoes running out barefoot, laughing and chuckling. At such times Miles would entice staff to follow or chase him, running off sneaking looks to see if adults were in pursuit.

Inclusive friendly places

Addressing physical modifications will not be enough; emotional changes requiring adults to make positive shifts and adopt inclusive opinions and philosophies will also be necessary.

> Accessibility is often determined as much by social inclusion and resourcefulness as by physical design. The attitudes of staff and management will be vital in determining whether a child with a disability feels included in any service and especially in the outdoor programme. Staff need to be conscious of the importance of outdoor play, and the value of nature and natural elements. Natural elements in an early childhood setting do not need to be on a grand scale. They can be quite small, but will make a big difference.
>
> (Jeavons, in Elliott, 2008: 129)

The thoughts of most parents of disabled children say 'they would rather their children encounter acceptable risk in play than be excluded' (ODPM, 2003: 39). Start your thoughts with 'we can do' and when faced with challenges ask others 'why not?' Partnership between parents, carers and practitioners will be essential to provide a shared understanding and opportunities for inclusive outdoor play. 'Time for play in childhood is linked to happiness in adulthood' (Rogers *et al.*, 2009) and children's 'stress levels fall within minutes of being outside' (National Wildlife Federation, 2010: 8) are both important research findings. Starting early and increasing the amount of time children play outside may have a profound impact on their levels of fitness and fun.

Everyone needs a shared interpretation when attempting to provide adventurous, exploratory and experiential inclusive outdoor play. In particular children with disabilities require a cohesive team to support and facilitate quality play in the outdoors and to help them to achieve their potential. Where successful inclusive

---

ENCOUNTER: Loving the outdoors

At the end of the woodland session this week, three different children all wanted to walk back to the site of their house for the mud men to show their parents. One dad had said previously that he felt so lucky that his son had the opportunity to play outside with us once a week; another collected her son and said they were off with toddler sister to some more woods to host a birthday party as he so loved being outdoors.

outdoor play is concerned everyone has a role and every child recognised as truly unique. Casey (2010: 30) is keen to point out that 'an inclusive play environment should be flexible enough to meet the play aspirations of the child rather than the child fitting the environment.' An important factor is the way the space 'makes children and families feel' (ODPM, 2003: 31). Asking children what they want and using their insights helps us to create inclusive friendly spaces. Where children are unable to speak for themselves, those who advocate on their behalf need to ensure that they are aware of the child's requirements and their interests. Experiences motivating and delighting children may at times be in opposition to that which adults may feel are necessities for children and providing for children's enjoyment without consideration of their safety may threaten their welfare and the affordance of outdoor experiences. Balancing the two is the challenge for adults supporting and providing a harmonious outside play environment. Enthusiastic practitioners should 'recognise, capture and share children's learning outdoors with parents and other people working with the child, so that they too become enthused' (White, 2008: 8).

Provocations

- When did you last crawl outside or walk the boundaries at child level? What can you see, hear and feel? Are there 'secret' areas where children can play, hide, discover and imagine? Are all the spaces and areas accessible to children and their carers?

- When you say it is too cold, too wet, too hot . . . is that for you or the children? Have an open conversation with your colleagues about what you honestly like and dislike about being outside with children and take a small step to open up some possibilities for yourself.

- Ask yourself what you know about approaches that support outdoor inclusive play, for instance Reggio Emilia or forest schooling. Think of common threads within these approaches. How might these approaches support and influence you to develop your own inclusive practice?

- How might your understanding of 'acceptable risk' compare to that of your colleagues or managers? What impact might these differences have on your ability to create inclusive outdoor environments?

- We show that play outdoors is *not* a case of replicating the indoors, '*taking the indoors out*' in principle, it is fundamentally different. Look at curriculum areas where you would feel confident to use the outdoors to support learning. Think also about areas of the curriculum where you might currently struggle, how you might develop your confidence and skill.

- Where do you find your inspiration to embrace inclusive outdoor play, how might you inspire, guide and empower others?

References

Banning, W. and Sullivan, G. (2011) *Lens on Outdoor Learning*, Minnesota, MN: Redleaf Press.

Bilton, H. (2010) *Outdoor Learning in the Early Years: Management and innovation*, London: Routledge.

Broadhead, P. and Burt, A. (2012) *Understanding Young Children's Learning through Play. Building Playful Pedagogies*, London: Routledge.

Casey, T. (2007) *Environments for Outdoor Play: A practical guide to making spaces for children*, London: Sage.

Casey, T. (2010) *Inclusive Play: Practical strategies for children from birth to eight*, 2nd edn, London: Sage.

Commission for Architecture and the Built Environment (CABE) (2010) *Community Green: Using local spaces to tackle inequality and improve health*, London: Cabe.

Davy, A. and Gallagher, J. (2006) *New Playwork: Play and care for children 4–16*, 4th edn, London: Thomson Learning Vocational.

Day, C. (2007) *Environment and Children. Passive Lessons From the Everyday Environment*, Oxford: Elsevier.

Dickins, M. and Denziloe, J. (2003) *All Together: How to create inclusive services for disabled children and their families*, 2nd edn, London: National Children's Bureau.

Education Act (1996) London: HMSO.

Gargiulo, R. M. and Kilgo, J. L. (2011) *An Introduction to Young Children with Special Needs Birth through Age Eight*, 3rd edn, California: Sage.

Garrick, R. (2009) *Playing Outdoors in the Early Years*, London: Continuum.

Great Britain. Parliament. *Disability Discrimination Act 2005*, London: HMSO.

Great Britain. Parliament. *Discrimination Act 2010*, London: HMSO.

Hart, S., Dixon, A., Drummond, M. J. and Mcintyre, D. (2004) *Learning without Limits*, Maidenhead, UK: Open University Press.

Jeavons, M. (2008) Chapter 6. Making Natural Playspaces More Accessible to Children with Disabilities. In: Elliott, S. (ed.). *The Outdoor Playspace Naturally For Children Birth to Five Years*. New South Wales: Pademelon Press.

Kane, E. W. (2006) No way my boys are going to be like that!, *Gender and Society*, 20: 149–76.

Kein, D., Cook, R. E. and Richardson-Gibbs, A. M. (2001) *Strategies for Including Children with Special Needs in Early Childhood Settings*, New York: Delmar-Thompson Learning.

Knight, S. (2011) *Risk and Adventure in Early Years Outdoor Play, Learning from Forest Schools*, London: Sage.

Lindon, J. (2001) *Understanding Children's Play*, Cheltenham, UK: Nelson Thomas.

Lindon, J. (2011) *Too Safe for Their own Good? Helping Children Learn about Risk and Lifeskills*, London: National Children's Bureau.

Ludvigsen, A., Creegan, C. and Mills, H. (2005) *Let's Play Together: Play and inclusion. Evaluation of Better Play Round Three*, Barkingside, UK: Barnardos.

Mills, A. and Gleave, J. (2010) *Playing Outdoors? Disabled Children's Views of Play Pathfinder and Playbuilder Play Spaces: An overview of KIDS research*, London: KIDS.

Nabors, L., Willoughby, J., Leff, S. and McMenamin, S. (2001) Promoting inclusion for young children with special needs on playgrounds, *Journal of Developmental and Physical Disabilities*, 13.2: 179–90.

National Wildlife Federation (2010) *Whole Child: Developing mind, body and spirit through outdoor play, VA (Canada)*. Available online at: www.nwf.org/Get-Outside/Be-Out-There/Why-Be-Out-There/Special-Reports/Whole-Child.aspx (accessed 4 July 12).

Nind, M., Rix, J., Sheehy, K. and Simmons, K. (2005) *Curriculum and Pedagogy in Inclusive Education: Values into practice*, Oxford: RoutledgeFalmer.

Office of the Deputy Prime Minister (ODPM) (2003) *Developing Accessible Play Space: A good practice guide*, London: ODPM. Available online at: www.communities.gov.uk/documents/communities/pdf/131052.pdf (accessed 4 July 12).

Ouvry, M. (2005) *Exercising Muscles and Minds: Outdoor play and the early years curriculum*, National Early Years Network, London.

Pellegrini, A. D. (2005) *Recess: Its role in education and development*, New Jersey: Lawrence Erlbaum.

Rogers, S., Pelletier, C. and Clark, A. (2009) Play and Outcomes for Children and Young People: Literature Review to Inform the National Evaluation of Play Pathfinders and Play Builders, *DCSFRBX-09-06*.

Tucker, F. and Matthews, H. (2001) They don't like girls hanging around there: conflicts over recreational space in rural Northamptonshire, *Area*, 33(2): 161–8.

United Nations (1989) *Convention on the Rights of the Child*. Available online at: www2.ohchr.org/english/law/crc.htm (accessed 19 March 2012).

White, J. (2008) *Playing and Learning Outdoors: Making provision for high-quality provision in the outdoor environment*, Oxford: Routledge.

Wilson, R. (2003) *Special Educational Needs in the Early Years*, 2nd edn, London: Routledge Falmer.

Wilson, R. (2008) *Nature and Young Children: Encouraging creative play and learning in natural environments*, Oxford: Routledge.

Wilson, R. (2012) *Nature and Young Children: Encouraging creative play and learning in natural environments*, 2nd edn. Oxford: Routledge.

Woods, A. (2016b) *Elemental Play and Outdoor Learning: Young children's playful connections with people, places and things*. London: Routledge.

Yelland, N. (2003) *Gender in Early Childhood*, London: Routledge.

Planning for risky possibilities in play

Cyndy Hawkins

The philosophical approach of this chapter is profoundly influenced by the writer and play commentator Bob Hughes who has inspired the field of playwork principles. We think early years workers can take much from his approach when regarding play opportunities. Rather than there being a divide in principles relating to children's play in playwork and early years play, there is a synergy when dealing with adventurous play scenarios. Historically, adults working with the early years have engaged in more precautionary principles in planning for physical encounters, though there is increasing evidence with influences such as forest school approaches that this is changing through acceptance that risk taking is a widespread and a fundamental psyche of children's play. Hughes (2012) describes the 'evolutionary nature of play', that is the notion that children have always engaged historically in wild environments and have survived, that human beings have always had to deal with risk and therefore taking risks is a normal part of children's development. Gray (2013: 119) concurs, 'from a biological/evolutionary perspective, play is nature's way of ensuring that young mammals including young humans, with practice can become good at the skills they need to develop and thrive on their own'. The normality of risk is however challenged by the potential danger of risk and it is the association between risk and danger that needs more clarification in order to aid adults' understanding, awareness and acceptance of risk as a normal rather than an abnormal undertaking in children's play. Danger emerges in risk taking when children's own recognition of risk is absent. It then becomes a hazard. Hughes remarks:

> I would define risk as those parts of the physical environment that the child is aware of, which if engaged with may result in physical injury. The important distinguishing feature of risk is that the child is aware the risk is there. Danger on the other hand, is when a child is unaware of the risk or the nature of it.
>
> (2012: 312)

This chapter is about encouraging adults to allow children to engage more in open play scenarios than they do at present and to promote confidence in adults to plan for opportunities to develop adventurous encounters in children's play. Through discussions in this chapter we hope to convince adults of the benefits of play while extinguishing possible false perceptions about safety requirements. Finally we hope to convert adults' beliefs about children's risk competencies that will enable them to have faith in their decision making to plan for more risky and adventurous possibilities in children's play.

Much of the current debate surrounding risk perceptions and risk practices consider how far it affects the adult role. Waite, Huggins and Wickett (in Maynard and Waters, 2014: 81) suggest that we

> have problemetised discourse around risk in relation to differing but contemporaneous conceptualizations of childhood, arguing that adopting a fixed view of the universal child fails to acknowledge the messiness and complexity of situated, cultural and individual responses to risk and security.

Here, we echo the narrative of the previous chapter and also consider some of the possibilities for engaging in planning for adventurous play, through a series of small encounters that are presented to provoke reflections on adults' current practices and importantly consideration for new approaches. We hope by embarking on this chapter it will offer some fresh approaches or provide some additional inspiration for planning to include more risk associated play spaces and materials for children in the early years. It is expected that the chapter will open up some of the mythology surrounding health and safety practices, which often limit what adults are prepared to allow children to engage with and spark a debate about the 'safe enough' principle versus the 'safety above' principle that influence current adult practices and interventions.

Allowing for risky encounters in play is quite a controversial topic and too often misunderstood by adults where organizational rules apply pressure on adults to minimize or eliminate experiences that involve physical risk taking with children. Organizations have rules about seen and unseen spaces, landscape terrains and materials, all presenting challenges for adults venturing into unknown territories and horizons in play practices; it is not just organizations, however, that put adults under pressure, pressure also comes from parents. As adults working with children we are guardians of children in our care *in loco parentis*, the benchmark for this is making judgments that a 'reasonable parent' would make, yet as Gill (2007: 63) points out, the parenting culture of today expects that someone is in charge and in control of their children most of the time, leading to high levels of supervision of children becoming the norm. The adult professional therefore is under dual pressure to accede to the demands of risk averse organizational rules and parental anxiety, rather than conferring to their own professional judgments. Risk averse cultures and perceptions provide unwilling conditions for how we plan for opportunities for children in their play. The dilemma currently for adults when planning any activity in a risk averse climate is that activities need to be for the benefit of the children, be stimulating and challenging, yet ensure a virtually zero risk result. A challenge of great magnitude! We need, therefore, to consider how we can provide a balance between safety and risk that will allow opportunities for children to engage with risk in what we will call a 'safe enough environment', within a well-managed risk framework.

It may be that your organization has already embarked on this course of action or perhaps is considering how to begin to offer more adventurous play scenarios, then the suggestions forthcoming in this chapter are for you to take as much or as little that you feel is appropriate. The decisions made about planning for possibilities in play and consequent risk and safety considerations will be dependent on the organization, the age of the children and the resources at hand. Decisions will also be guided and governed by the culture and philosophy of the organization, perceptions and approaches to risk management practices. Risk taking is not watching a child growing in confidence as they climb a tree; risk taking is being willing to be in the woods in the first place.

Recognition and awareness of risk therefore are somewhat predetermined by a child's knowledge and experience of a situation that will drive or exclude them from an activity based on their level of confidence and awareness. From this knowledge we advocate the first principle for planning for adventurous play is the importance of children's autonomy in decision making as a prerequisite for adopting appropriate behaviours in play activities; it appears crucial for children's development in self-regulation. Allowing children autonomy for decision making in play is uppermost, as when we observe risky play situations we do not always know the potential a child has in controlling the risky situation. This is because we are not inside the child's head, in control of their thought processes, nor necessarily able to gauge their capabilities. Second, observing children taking risks can lead us to suppose a situation incorrectly and this may not always be appropriate or beneficial to the child's experiences as it could limit the threshold of their abilities. In play situations, therefore, children need to learn to adapt and cope in different environments and it is crucial that they learn through autonomous risk taking to deal with and control risks independent of adults' interventions. Letting go is not an easy undertaking for adults and as such responsibility in risk taking in play is becoming a more difficult objective for children to achieve. Risk aversion per se increases adults' fears of the consequences of their decision making and possible litigations, quelling adult urges to consider diverse planning practices. This is further evident in adult concerns over children's well-being and safety that has been elevated by negative reports in the media and amplification of risk and safety occurrences. Consequently children are being denied access to engage in activities that carry any element of risk taking (Furedi, 1997). In conclusion, the *normality* of risk taking in play has been hindered by media hype and by adult misconceptions about health and safety regulations where safety concerns have outweighed risk gains. Debate around children and safety has prioritized and centred on the dominance of safety considerations in play and through this agenda has functioned to curtail adults' practices in planning. This has resulted in children missing opportunities for negotiating freely with risks. The following discussion will show evidence for young children displaying risk competence and as such should give confidence to adults to allow both opportunities for risk taking and autonomy.

The absence of risk negotiations and challenges in play for children cannot be understated, as without opportunities to make decisions independent of the adult reduces children's potential development. Vygotsky's (1978) zone of proximal development discusses learning possibilities when children are supported by others more experienced than them, but more importantly the zone demonstrates what children can do alone, their potential, which is guided by their instincts and independent decision making.

In our experience, children will climb trees that they assess they *can* climb; they can be encouraged to consider whether they will be able to climb down on their own before starting up. My advice to them before climbing would always be, 'look to see how you will climb down'.

Christensen and Mikkelsen (2008) suggest that children do carefully assess risks based on self-perception and their own physical abilities. Stephenson (2003), while

---

ENCOUNTER: The lying tree

Our first visit to the millennium woodland to assess the environment for pre-school forest school highlighted that all the trees were immature; very few were over fifteen foot high and were of species that had not yet developed low, climbable branches. There was a larger open space at the lower end of the wood, surrounded by piles of coppiced branches and small trees. We identified a few that may offer the possibility of climbing. At the first session, twins quickly identified a tree with branches low enough to get a foot up and proceeded to get four or five feet off the ground. They then managed to lie on a branch and look upwards at the sky. The tree was named the 'lying tree' by the boys and became a target for all the children as they started each session.

ENCOUNTER: With stairs

From becoming a mobile baby around nine months to around five years of age, a child was always accompanied up and down stairs, to prevent and avoid falling down the stairs. Stair gates were in place throughout these years. The child, by six years of age, was not confident of independently negotiating the stairs.

A generation later, a child of nine months, now secure in his crawling is encouraged to climb up the stairs and taught to turn round and come backwards down the stairs, using his hands to slow or speed up the process. As soon as he could walk, his father waited patiently while he climbed the stairs and came back down again many times until the child was competent and independent and safe on the stairs.

observing young children under two, found evidence that even young children display risk competence and that risky activities were actually integral to extending young children's physical prowess.

May, Ashford and Bottle (2006: 51) claim

> if a child is to grow into a self-assured adult, then one of the important aspects of their progress is the development of movement. This is part of growing up, as the child not only learns about their own physical capability but also learns about their own existence in space, their place in the physical world and the relationships between themselves and others.

Senniger (2000) describes the process of risk taking in children as the 'learning zone model', akin to Vygotsky's zone of proximal development; risk competency is a journey that happens step by step where gradually children leave the comfort of the zone to undertake more and more challenging pursuits. In the previous encounters, it is argued that risk adversity has created an environment of low confidence and incompetence, resulting in a possible accident outside the everyday context and the second encounter more likely to support the child's management of risk. Gill (2007, cited in Knight, 2011: 4) argues that this learning is crucial in

1 Helping children to learn how to manage risk (understanding safety).
2 Feeding children's innate need for risk with reasonable risks in order to prevent them finding greater unmanaged risks for themselves.
3 Health and development benefits.
4 The building of character and personality traits such as resilience and self-reliance.

Any planning for play needs to consider the adult's role and the child's competencies in play situations and secondly, the benefits attached in allowing for more autonomous risk taking in play to take place. Further principles underpinning fresh approaches in planning for play are related to the rules we attach to environments, materials and the amount of freedom children are allowed in their play.

Developmentally the physical and psychological challenges of risk-taking in play benefit the child's overall well-being through deep immersion, concentration and involvement in their play (Laevers, 1997). Concentration and involvement in play encourage deep play scenarios, which are particular attributes needed for creative and adventurous play encounters, as challenge to the self is the main objective in risk-taking. Play further encourages and stimulates children's mental and physical faculties through demands on all of their sensory and physical attributes such as vision, touch and awareness, each key to risky pursuits. Further research suggests that play acts as a scaffold for development for increasing children's neural structures. Neuroscientists suggest children consciously seek out uncertainty both physically and emotionally in their play and that uncertainty in play situations not only helps to shape children's emotions, as they experience things such as fear and exhilaration, but that uncertainty also fuels the motivation and reward regions in the brain providing the impetus for more discovery learning (see Sutton-Smith, 2003; Burghardt, 2005). On an emotional level challenging scenarios bring out a range of emotions that Damasio (2003) recalls as raw primary emotions including fear, anger, surprise and disgust needed for risky types of play; it also encourages resilience building in children, through children operating in adverse conditions testing their resistance and tenacity to succeed. It would appear, therefore, that children are wired naturally to seek out challenges to test their boundaries and aptitudes so that they can continue to progress their responses and adaptations to diverse and challenging conditions. Adults working with children should not fear or fight children's natural compulsion to 'be dizzy' and take risks, rather they should embrace it for the advantages it presents.

Planning for risky possibilities in play more often requires a cultural change in risk management practices, attitudes towards risk, and the offer of play materials. It also requires a more moderate course of action between the amount of control and autonomy children are necessitated. Newstead (2008) argues that adults often take a 'nuclear approach' to risk taking by completely stopping children from doing things for fear of the 'what if syndrome'; 'what if' being a negative connotation aligned with fear of the consequences of risky play leading to accidents or being sued, as we have suggested earlier. It is our contention that it is the fear of litigation that is one of the main factors that prevent the more adventurous play activities being offered to children. Adults are so concerned with assessing risk that they miss the fundamental point of establishing risk, which is the relationship between the human ability to recognize risk and their resilience to it, not the risk itself. An adult's responsibility is to demonstrate reasonable practicability and safe enough practices, not the elimination of all risks, changing 'what if' into a positive implication. Knight (2011: 106–7) highlights the concept of risk-benefit as opposed to risk-aversion in her five-step process:

1 Identify the hazards.
2 Decide who might be harmed and how.
3 Evaluate the risks and decide on your actions and precautions.
4 Record your findings and implement them.
5 Review your risk assessment.

She cites the DfES (2007) who talk about 'reasonable risk taking' (practice card 1.4, EYFS), suggesting that

the responsible adult has recognized the risk, examined the hazards, balanced the likelihood of an accident happening, against the severity of the harm that would take place if it happened, and taken the appropriate action. What is left is an experience where the risk is reasonable for the age and stage of the children taking part in it.

(Knight, 2011: 103)

Treasure baskets are a good example here of offering babies and toddlers an interesting array of objects to explore in their own ways and own time, with observant adults watching to see how they react, what they choose, what they return to and 'treasure' and what they reject due to the feel, shape or taste. Very young children develop their sensory schemas through treasure basket play, making connections between the feel and look of shiny objects, natural objects, objects that roll, objects that fit into other objects, and objects that make a noise. None of the objects are bought toys but observing the babies' and toddlers' concentration should help us see that perhaps the narrowness of some of the 'safe' choices we make by rejecting materials marketed for over threes only. We are not advocating unsafe objects, which are sharp, small enough to swallow or easily breakable, but a pastry brush, a balloon whisk and a set of linking chains fascinate little ones and can be three of the objects in a treasure basket.

Making positive choices such as avoiding potentially toxic materials like glitter or polystyrene with little babies who will always test things out in their mouths, their most developed muscles, is not the same as safely introducing scissors and tools when the children are able to understand how to use them carefully themselves. We should not deny our children the opportunity to be independent, creative, mechanical, design and makers, using hammers, screwdrivers, saws, secateurs and scissors as part of their everyday experience.

Tovey (2007) explains this shift in risk relationships from risk assessment, to 'resilience and skills to be safe', with the introduction of safety and planning audits embedded into the play process, to *allow* for risky possibilities to happen rather than prevent it. The environment should be safe, 'safe to take risks not safe from risk'. This can be achieved through planning that allows for the use of diverse terrains, materials and encounters to be experienced in a safe enough environment – and here we can interpret risk as *possibility*. In this chapter we aim to inform how the reflective role of adults in planning and evaluating risky play provision is crucial and can help to sustain and promote increased possibilities for risky play. Building on Chapter 4, exploiting outdoor possibilities, this chapter focuses particularly on risky play environments, particularly those afforded by the outdoors. We begin with exploring 'what if?'

When adults begin to plan for risky possibilities in play they can start by taking a fresh look at the physical environment, such as the amount of space and objects being used and the types of vistas there are in the vicinity. Adults should try to envisage how the environment might offer possibilities for children to engage in a variety of play scenarios using the landscape outdoors and the space indoors as tools. No matter how many or few scenarios, adults should consider how children might use materials and space; ultimately adults will never be able to imagine or create as much as the children will eventually produce. The uncertainty of not knowing the eventualities of how children might engage with the environment is to be tolerated. In terms of planning for risky possibilities, the focus is more on the *affordances* that the environment or particular outdoor resources might produce such as climbing, sliding, balancing, jumping, hiding, using an old tree stump, log or rock. Significantly the performances of children using the spaces and interacting with materials determine the actions and interactions with the environment that stimulates opportunities for greater diversity in play, allowing for risk taking to emerge. The most important consideration in planning for risky play is that adults stimulate a fresh approach in considering spaces and materials across the landscape, particularly variations of height and depth.

In play possibilities, varied topographies in landscapes are essential as Gibson (1977) states when considering flat empty spaces, that they offer 'few affordances' for types of play that have an element of risk attached, therefore to begin with, adults need to ensure that the environmental landscape is varied enough for children to try out their physical skills and attributes such as strength, balance, coordination, flexibility and endurance, while supporting children's mental capacities of spatial awareness and problem solving through different terrains. Accommodating indeterminable terrains means adopting spaces and materials that will challenge uncertainty and harness potential development through pushing children's physical, mental and geographic boundaries. For adults, extending spaces and places of different heights and depths in the environment may require access to former limited geographic and mental boundaries and the establishment of additional challenging topographies. The following table gives a summary of the variety of landscape features that have been considered by contemporary authors.

It may remind us that a flat concrete or tarmac surface increases a risk of children running, falling or being pushed over, and that an expanse of grass encourage boisterous ball play where the same may happen. Minor accidents happen every-where and in every context, including in cramped classrooms where tables, chairs and equipment have to be negotiated.

Table 5.1 Outdoor surfaces to be considered

Slopes, hillocks; grassy banks; mounds; uneven ground	Casey, 2007; Garrick, 2011; Young, 2011; Watts, 2011; Tovey, 2011, 2013
Hollows	Casey, 2007
Corners	Watts, 2011
Soft matting	Garrick, 2011
Pathways; grass/herb pathway; winding tracks	Garrick, Young, 2011
Bark chippings	Bilton, 2005
Slabs	Garrick, 2011
Stepping stones	Garrick, Curtis & Carter, 2003; Watts, 2011
Tunnels	Garrick, 2011; Tovey, 2011
Ditches	Tovey, 2011, 2013
Soft earth	Spencer & Blades, 2006
Boulders	Casey, 2007
Small pebbles; gravel	Bilton, 2005
Uneven ground	Watts, 2011; Tovey, 2013
Arches; Pergolas	Young, 2011

Source: Woods, 2016b: 124

Approaching planning in this new open-ended way can initially be a challenge, but once considered, the benefits of allowing more variation in topographical experiences for children brings with it richness, diversity of actions and attitudes and immense possibilities for children. It is important, too, to look at the spaces you create indoors for flexible, indoor play encounters as suggested in Chapter 1. Have a look to see where children might be able to move loose equipment/resources safely; consider the secret, playful places that children like to use to talk and be imaginative; carry out an audit of ground level and table level activity, and the space for easy movement between obstacles. A 'child high' crawl through your indoor space may illuminate opportunities that could be created.

Decisions children make when they interact with challenging landscapes begin in the child's mind, not the adult's mind, with questions such as: What should I do with this? How can I use it? Will I fall, get trapped? Can I escape? Am I strong enough, tall enough, small enough to push, reach, squeeze? Will I succeed in the challenges this object/terrain presents?

These are questions and challenges that adults cannot plan for, as each individual child will use spaces and materials in quite unique ways. *Planning for these possible questions appears to be the key here.* Children learn to cope and manipulate the environment; they learn how to be part of it, how to work with it and against it, but overall to master and control it. Physical landscapes that offer a variance in topographies allow children to experience different levels of discrete sized spaces and numerous imaginative encounters to inspire their creativity and imagination through their physical and mental senses. Changing topographies in an environment can be a challenge and not without some hesitation and reluctance shown by adults who can provoke doubt and concern. Children need to encounter terrains of different height and weight underfoot, manipulating natural and manmade materials; they need to experience height and movement from slow and steady pace to fast and exhilarating pace. Through the use of different landscapes and objects set at ground and above ground level, children learn to negotiate with terrains that react and behave in different ways. In these more challenging play

ENCOUNTER: A small child

A rare but rewarding time in a nursery classroom really opened my eyes to the 'small enough spaces'. A three-year-old, with what his parents defined as primordial dwarfism, was incredibly clever at avoiding helping out at tidy up time. As soon as he became aware of the music/bubbles, and that each child had a task to help everyone, he would go and find the smallest space underneath, behind and in, where he knew we would not find him, let alone reach in to encourage him out. He alerted us to the more dangerous places where he might hide (and get stuck). We looked with different eyes at our indoor and outdoor environment.

activities, a small accident may happen, perhaps a little scrape, a minor fall, a tiny knock; these events are not necessarily a bad thing as this is how children learn to re-negotiate with objects, learning to use them more successfully and effectively. Adults, at this stage of development in their play environment, must decide on balance that when offering more challenging encounters for children they consider carefully whether the benefits outweigh the risks. This is a professional judgment call. Hughes (2006) advocates that the 'world is full of rules' and that we need freedom to try out new experiences. Many of the benefits of limiting unnecessary rules in play is that it allows for children's extension of physical, mental and emotional attributes. To consolidate the dilemma of risk and possible injury, it is imperative for adults working with children to legitimize minor injuries through their organizational policies and practices, explaining to parents that lessons learned early on in life can save children from more damaging injuries later as they learn about their strengths, weaknesses and capabilities (see for example Ball, 2002; Gill, 2007; Hughes, 2012). Legitimizing minor injuries in children's play requires adults to adopt a bold and pioneering approach to risk, planning for risky possibilities that may result occasionally in a minor injury, but overall the benefits exhort positive and powerful advantages for children's well-being and development. Unpredictable terrains in the physical landscape provide a chance to test and experience risk in ways that otherwise would not be experienced. Terrains of this nature also provide new challenges for adults as uneven vistas promote areas that are not always visible.

Children's space and personal geographies and freedoms are constantly being squeezed (see Matthews *et al.*, 1999; Geldens and Bourke, 2008). Additionally children's access to private space is under threat because of implied safety considerations. Children in their play and movements are continually under surveillance under the banner of health and safety (see Furedi, 1997; Ball, 2002; Gill, 2007). There is an implicit fear of leaving children alone and unattended. The consequences of continued surveillance for children and adults compromise freedom in children's play. Hughes (2001: 344) argues to be hidden is a 'play necessity and being overlooked [by adults] takes something valuable away from play . . ., children need to have time to make decisions'.

Materials: fixed or loose?

Choosing materials for play opportunities requires consideration of the type of materials to offer and these can be divided into two distinct groups. Fixed play materials include things that stay static such as swings or climbing frames and loose play materials comprise pieces of materials such as tubes or ropes that can be moved and combined with static play equipment or with other loose parts for children to invent their own constructions. The benefits of using loose parts successfully stems from the work of Nicholson (1971: 30) who discovered that when children have opportunities to 'use lots of variables' in their play (materials) they use them in much more imaginative and creative ways: 'in any environment both the degree of inventiveness and creativity and the possibility of discovery are directly proportional to the number and kinds of variables in it.' The materials within the environment should be aligned to sustainable spaces where children can change and alter play activities to suit their interests and motivations using both static and loose materials. Children's ability to modify and manipulate their environment is crucial for inspiration and creativity and so that play spaces do not become stale. The element of surprise and unpredictability of using loose parts helps to satisfy children's imagination and creativity. This process of learning is strongly evident in Malaguzzi's (1993) approach in Reggio Emilia, where loose parts are used in indoor and outdoor learning environments to touch, move, explore and express with, and has been extensively researched by Broadhead and Burt (2012).

Creating risky possibilities with loose materials enables children to find more novel ways to use everyday objects in unique and inspirational ways. The template of this approach in the provision of materials is to promote more of an adventure playground feel than a school playground to progress the use of materials that promote risky possibilities. The emphasis in planning is to combine interesting and stimulating materials that will stretch, challenge and provide enjoyable opportunities for children to explore and discover with. Both natural and manufactured materials can be mixed and work well for children to experiment with. Inspiration for outdoor play materials and risky encounters can be drawn from the use of elements and materials that we find in the natural world. Play materials can include, rock, fire, air, earth, plants, water, wood, rope and motion vehicle activities (Hughes, 1996). Elemental materials (see Woods, 2016b) are fully endorsed in forest school approaches and outdoor learning where children are allowed to reconnect with nature using predominately natural materials to extend their learning and skills.

Pioneers such as McMillan (1919) advocated the benefits of the outdoors as a learning vehicle as it was seen to stimulate opportunities to develop particularly sensory awareness through smell, touch, sound, taste, sight and also physical development through engaging with elements and materials in unique and individual ways. Imagination and creativity are enhanced when thought provoking loose parts are embedded into children's play.

Loose parts promote both boisterous play activities and solitary play. The main characteristics in loose play are interactions with others and the parts. It is often excitable play with lots of shouting and movement. Parts tend to change hands regularly, either voluntarily or sometimes grasped by another child who envisages that part in their own interpretations and representations. Loose parts used in play produce free flow, fluid activities, where interconnections with parts and persons provide encounters and relationships that promote risk because of the fast pace, unpredictability and imagination to take on new roles expanding children'shorizons. A very good example of loose play in practice is the introduction of 'scrapstore playpods' in school playgrounds to promote positive social interactions in playgrounds (Blatchford et al., 2002). The scrapstore is a large outdoor storage area where a collection of loose scrap materials are stored and in outdoor play the children choose items to play with. Where scrapstores have been used successfully, observations show that play becomes more purposeful, as children focus their attention and efforts more on creativity and using their imagination where the parts act as symbolic representations in their play. Benefits for planning by developing a scrapstore of loose parts is that it appears to reduce conflict and encourages cooperation between children where there are enough parts for all the children to have something to handle. Additionally children tend to find loose part play

Table 5.2 Loose materials for play

Sand	Hay & Nye, 1996; Edgington, 2002; Bilton, 2005; Casey, 2007; Williams-Siegfredson, 2012
Gravel	Bilton, 2005
Water	Hay & Nye, 1996; Edgington, 2002; Bilton, 2005
Small pebbles	Edgington, 2002; Curtis & Carter, 2003; Bilton, 2005; Broadhead & Burt, 2012
Tall grasses	Garrick, 2011
Small trees and shrubs	Garrick, 2011
Twigs and branches	Curtis & Carter, 2003; Spencer & Blades, 2006; Garrick, 2011; Broadhead & Burt, 2012
Seedheads, conkers, acorns, cones	Edgington, 2002; Curtis & Carter, 2003; Garrick, 2011
Soil/mud	Greenman, 1988; Hay & Nye, 1996; Spencer & Blades, 2006; Williams-Siegfredson, 2012; Broadhead & Burt, 2012
Logs	Edgington, 2002; Watts, 2011
Rocks and stones	Day, 2007; Young, Watts, 2011
Planter boxes	Young, 2011
Hanging baskets	Edgington, 2002
Crystals	Day, 2007
Flowers	Greenman, 1988
Composting	Elliott, 2008
Worm farms	Elliott, 2008
Animals	Elliott, 2008
Wooden house, toadstool table and stools	Garrick, 2011
Willow tunnel	Garrick, 2011
Wigwam	Garrick, 2011
Bark	Greenman, 1988; Edgington, 2002; Bilton, 2005; Garrick, 2011
Haybales	Curtis & Carter, 2003
Boulders	Curtis & Carter, 2003; Young, 2011
Shells	Edgington, 2002; Ryder, nd
Tree stumps	Maxwell et al., 2008

Source: Woods, 2016b: 113

ENCOUNTER: It's this . . . it's that . . . it's this . . .

Adults leave a selection of loose parts in the play area to observe the children's reactions. At first the children circle the parts and then slowly each child begins to choose a part to pick up and play with. A plastic bucket is a hat and then a drum and then a podium, then two buckets become handbags and then builders' buckets and then a pair of boots. A long length of thick twig is a whiplash, then a sword to fight with, then a fairy wand, then an arrow, then a flying horse. Hessian sacks are used to collect plants for dinner, then a hiding place to stow a magic cloak and a jumping jack to jump around in, tripping over and getting up again.

ENCOUNTER: You spin me round . . .

Climbing up the rocky slope, Karis dangles a long, flowing ribbon tail behind her, looking back each time she takes a step further up the slope. She lets the ribbon ripple over the stones until she reaches the grass platform, where she pulls herself up to standing position. Turning now backward facing, she takes four deliberate steps across the grassy bank waving the ribbon like a snake in front of her. It is a windy day and the wind picks the ribbon up in the breeze. As with nature, Karis lets her arms take the breeze with the ribbon. Arms outstretched she closes her eyes and begins to turn in a circle but loses her balance momentarily, laughs and opens her eyes. She senses her limitations and begins instead to twirl the ribbon rather than her body, waving the ribbon around and around in large extended circular movements.

---

experiences more satisfying because they are able to shape and control objects in their play and encounter more freedom promoting the autonomous link to risky play possibilities. Adults' roles in loose part play are to remain again on the periphery as attuned observers rather than interventionists. Opportunity for risky possibilities are where the children begin to use parts to express not only their ideas but their emotions. As the play process is open-ended there are many possibilities for diverse contact with materials and relationships. Moving between materials and across the landscape, numerous physical motions are established throughout play, while the children control some of their experience, it is often the out-of-control sensations that motivate risky, *creative* play.

Pace, speed, height and motion

Perhaps the most risky encounters occur when children are involved in motion or height activities and it is usually when adults supervising children become most anxious. Typical solitary motion activities we remember as children were twirling activities, where we experienced dizzy swirling sensations in our heads that made us feel out of control yet were exhilarating. It is the sense of letting go momentarily, being out of control, that children naturally seek in physical play, because they are testing the boundaries of their senses and feelings. When we think about motion activities we think about actions associated with motions, such as rocking, spinning, swaying, propelling, height and place. Examples of motion play include activities where children go up, down, around and under. Experiences of speed include fast pace, slow pace and intermittent paces of fast and slow. Motion challenges are things that bring about feelings and attributes of courage, resilience, thrill and fear in children. An analogy of this is if we think about fairground rides – all designed to take motion, height and speed to the outer limits to deliberately evoke sensory and emotional reactions.

The types of traditional play materials typically offered for motion activities are bikes, scooters, slides, seesaws, roundabouts and climbing frames, with many settings having some examples of these. However, Hughes (2001: 345) argues 'that this is a convenient form of play, a fast food approach where children's natural play drives are hijacked by synthetic substitutes to produce stereotypical play narratives'. Hughes (2001: 387) goes on to argue we should be encouraging more free range playing. Free range playing involves what Hughes calls wild play where children are very much left to play instinctively with their environment without too much adult intervention or supervision. Hughes asserts that most synthetic materials such as bikes or climbing frames are used by children in a standardized way and do not offer the wider challenges to become masters in negotiating with metamorphic materials. Danish landscape architect Nebelong also rejects standardization in using materials, arguing in fact it can create its own dangers.

> When the distance between all rungs in a climbing net or ladder is exactly the same, the child has no need to concentrate on where he puts his feet. Standardisation is dangerous because play becomes simplified and the child does not have to worry about his movements. This lesson cannot be carried over to all the knobbly and asymmetrical forms with which one is confronted throughout life.
>
> (Nebelong 2002, cited in Gill, 2007: 35)

In planning for play possibilities adults are charged with providing materials and encounters that provide uncertainty and challenge in a safe way. Choice of motion, speed and height materials to allow for free range wild play scenarios require natural and or unregulated materials so rope swings, hammocks, rocky crevices, curved slopes could be alternatives to provide motion, height and speed experiences that can be used and effected in different ways. Free form (not fixed) equipment provide opportunities for children to negotiate, test, try out, conquer or fail in their pursuits, going back and trying again, building confidence, resilience and self-esteem. Further free form play establishes and increases children's cognitive maps and the way that they make sense of their worlds through familiarity and change, assimilating their experience through a different *dance* each time and thus accommodating memories to exploit in the next engagement.

Through the adaptations of motion play materials that support uncertainty, children act on and with the environment forming new perspectives and interpretations about materials and their environment. Through fresh experiences and interconnections children make sense of their worlds and begin to understand that materials and physical bodies can behave in unpredictable ways.

Transforming and sustaining risky play possibilities

The transformation and modification of the play environment and materials required for adventurous play possibilities arise from the adults' provision and evaluation of materials and environment and from the unique ways that the child interacts and connects with it. Play is an unfolding process, unpredictable, uncertain, evolutionary, because of the many facets that can develop, but key to all of this are the mental capacities required both of the adult and the child.

To sustain success and safety, adults and children need to reflect, evaluate and adapt to changing situations. Adults do this by observing the environment and materials and by looking at the possible opportunities and risk that they may present. Adults assess, modify and change structures to provide more challenge and more interest, and then let things develop in an organic evolutionary way. Children's behaviour mirrors this in that they too observe how they can use the environment and materials. They assess, modify, adapt and change the use of materials and landscapes to suit their purposes and imagination by creating and recreating new and expanding situations. Along the way children challenge their own capacities and abilities and take risks in order to develop and progress. It is this part of the transformative process that the adult must mirror from the child if they want to plan for creative possibilities in play. This part of the transformation process will come from challenging current ideas about the organization's environment, extending the capacities of the environment and taking risks in order to develop and progress. Continued reflection and evaluation of play provision through the planning process will help to sustain a stimulating and accessible environment for children where they will be afforded space, time, freedom and materials to pursue their individual challenges through risk and resilience strategies. Though this might prove unfamiliar territory for adults initially, the benefits and freedom afforded by both adult and child will open up new perspectives and confidence to manage more risks. Finally, keep in mind the safe enough principle, safe to do, not safe from, celebrating that the child is a capable being, capable to take risks and challenges in their play.

Provocations

- How would you define your organization's attitude towards risk and safety: are there lots of rules and restrictions regarding play?

- Would you consider or do you already have a policy or statement legitimizing minor injuries in play?

- Do you or your colleagues fully understand actual health and safety requirements versus some of the mythologies?

- How confident are you or your colleagues in letting go of the control of children in their play?

- What are the main barriers you perceive in planning for adventurous play and how might you overcome them?

- Does your outdoor environment have different terrains, hidden spaces, natural motion vehicles, abundant loose parts?

- Are your children 'free rangers' or 'bubble wrapped'?

References

Ball, D. J. (2002) *Playgrounds – Risks, Benefits and Choices*. London: Health and Safety Executive, Middlesex University.

Blatchford, P., Pellegrini, T., Baines, E. and Kentaro, K. (2002) *Playground Games: Their social context in elementary/junior school. Final Report to the Spencer Foundation 2002*. Available online at: www.breaktime.org.uk/SpencerFinalReport02.pdf (accessed March 2012).

Broadhead, P. and Burt, A. (2012) *Understanding Young Children's Learning through Play. Building Playful Pedagogies*. London: Routledge.

Burghardt, G. M. (2005) *The Genesis of Animal Play: Testing the limits*. Cambridge, MA: The MIT Press.

Christensen, P. and Mikkelsen, M. R. (2008) Jumping off and being careful: Children's strategies of risk management in everyday life. *Sociology of Health & Illness*, 30(1): 112–30.

Damasio, A. (2003) *Looking for Spinoza*. London: Heinemann.

Furedi, F. (1997) *Culture of Fear*. London: Continuum.

Geldens, P. and Bourke, L. (2008) Identity, uncertainty and responsibility: Privileging space in a risk society. *Children's Geographies*, 6(3): 281–94.

Gibson, J. J. (1977) The Theory of Affordances. In: R. Shaw and J. Bransford (eds). *Perceiving, Acting, and Knowing: Toward an ecological psychology* (pp. 67–82). Hillsdale, NJ: Lawrence Erlbaum.

Gill, T. (2007) *No Fear: Growing up in a risk averse society*. London: Calouste Gulbenkian Foundation.

Gray, P. (2013) *Free to Learn. Why Unleashing the Instinct to Play Will Make Our Children Happier, More Self-Reliant and Better Students for Life*. New York: Basic Books.

Hughes, B. (1996) *Play Environments: A question of quality*. London: PLAYLINK.

Hughes, B. (2001) *The First Claim, A Framework for Playwork Quality Assessment*. Cardiff, UK: Play Wales.

Hughes, B. (2006) *Play Types: Speculations and possibilities*. London: LNCPET.

Hughes, B. (2012) *Evolutionary Playwork*, 2nd edn. London: Routledge.

International Play Conference (2011) *Playing into the Future – Surviving and Thriving*. Proceedings of the IPA conference, 4–7 July 2011. Cardiff, UK: Cardiff University.

Knight, S. (2011) *Risk and Adventure in Early Years Outdoor Play. Learning from Forest Schools*. London: Sage.

Laevers. F. (1997) *A Process-orientated Child Monitoring System for Young Children*. Leuven: Centre for Experiential Education.

McMillan, M. (1999) *The Nursery School*. London: J. M. Dent & Sons.

Malaguzzi, L. (1993) History, ideas and basic philosophy. In: C. Edwards, L. Gandini and G. Forman (eds). *The Hundred Languages Children: The Reggio Emilia approach to early childhood education*. Norwood: Ablex.

Matthews, H., Limb, M. and Taylor, M. (1999) Reclaiming the Streets: The discourse of curfew. Environments and Planning, *Area*, 31(10) 17: 3–30.

May, P., Ashford, E. and Bottle, G. (2006) *Sound Beginnings: Learning and development in the early years*. London: Routledge.

Newstead, S. (2008) *The Buskers Guide to Risk*. Eastleigh, UK: Common Threads Publications.

Nicholson, S. (1971) How not to cheat children – the theory of loose parts. *Landscape Architecture*, 62: 30–5.

Stephenson, A. (2003) Physical risk-taking: Dangerous or endangered? *Early Years*. 23(1): 35–43.

Sutton-Smith, B. (2003) Play as a parody of emotional vulnerability. In J. L. Roopnarine (ed.). *Play and Educational Theory and Practice, Play and Culture Studies 5*. Westport, CT: Praeger.

Tovey, H. (2007) *Playing Outdoors: Spaces and places, risk and challenge*. Maidenhead, UK: McGraw-Hill Open University Press.

Vygoysky, L. S. (1978) Mind in society. In: Cole, M., John-Steiner, V., Scribner, S. and Souberman, E. (eds). *The Development of Higher Psychological Processes*. Cambridge: Harvard University Press.

Waite, S. Huggins, V. and Wickett, K. (2014) Chapter 5. Risky Outdoor Play: Embracing uncertainty in pursuit of learning. In Maynard, T. and Waters, J. (eds). *Exploring Outdoor Play in the Early Years*. Maidenhead, UK: OUP.

Woods, A. (2016b) *Elemental Play and Outdoor Learning: Young children's playful connections with people, places and things*. London: Routledge.

CHAPTER

6

Play as a space for possibilities

Moira Moran and Victoria Brown

In this chapter we will consider the importance of play for children, and some of its key characteristics. Moyles (2010: 4) describes the complexities of discussing play as similar to 'trying to seize bubbles', brilliantly capturing the fascinating, fragile and transitory nature of play. Challenging though it may be, it is worthwhile for practitioners to be able to discuss play authoritatively. As practitioners appreciative of the value of play for children and knowledgeable of its benefits, we will be confident to advocate for ample play opportunities for the children in our care.

Book after book and article upon article have been written on play, providing a wealth of opinions that indicate the value of play for children's holistic learning and development. It can be a hard task to find reference to adverse aspects of play or authors who do not find positive value in it. Yet we can face challenges when providing the practice and environments that enable play, as other pressures impact on our pedagogy, as the newly qualified teacher in a reception class notes in Encounter: Practitioner reflection.

Convinced of the benefits, in this particular context, the practitioner is able to implement a curriculum that she feels is right for her children as she has the full

---

ENCOUNTER: Practitioner reflection

There are challenges . . . I do feel restricted sometimes . . . I have to cover this . . . they need to do that . . . we haven't done any writing this week. It would be good to play more, do something more spontaneous. Our children are low down on the profile and so we feel we have to do more, to boost them up. That's why I do so much play too; because they need space to be children, pirates, superman, a mummy or a dog. . . . It is not *just* playing, they are not *only* playing. They are socialising, they are problem solving, they are exploring their emotions, making meaning, communicating, mark making, making decisions, building foundations. I am lucky here I don't have to fight for it.

95

support of the school leadership team who can see the value of play for their children. Despite this, however, she does at times feel her pedagogy is challenged, in particular by the curricular frameworks. Research reveals that practitioners can be theoretically convinced of the benefits of play, but less confident in how to implement those theories in their practice (Adams 2004 in Santer *et al.* 2007 and Moyles and Worthington 2011). As practitioners we clearly need to be able to practice what we preach; without the support of the whole setting this continues to provide a challenge.

The rhetoric and reality of play

Article 31 of the United Nations Convention on the Rights of the Child (UNCRC), ratified by the United Kingdom in 1991, recognises: 'the right of the child to rest and leisure, to engage in play and recreational activities appropriate to the age of the child' (UN, 1989). Ratification of the Act has impacted on increasingly wide areas of policy and practice since 1991, and play has been placed firmly at the heart of provision for children. For the youngest children, play has been identified as a most appropriate activity, and is advocated as such to practitioners. Strandell (2000) argues that the perspective on play as a child's right has, in Western society, become a channel through which to marginalise play as an activity particular to children, and through which to trivialise play and players. She problematises Western society's preschool pedagogy in which play is seen as a preparation and practice for a *future* reality, and adult–planned purposeful play becomes an essential ingredient in the mix for school readiness. In contrast she proposes a model of play as a construction and negotiation of *present* meaning. This model would suggest that if we can focus on the children who are in our settings now, can ensure that we offer them enriching and enabling experiences and opportunities meaningful to their present being and can join them as partners in play when appropriate then surely we are offering them the best preparation for the future that we can. As Groos wrote, describing how young animals' play experiences help them to develop: 'Youth probably exists for the sake of play. Animals cannot be said to play because they are young and frolicsome, *but rather have a period of youth in order to play*' (1808: 75).

Within frameworks and guidance for children in settings, play can be talked about principally as a medium for development and learning. This dominant discourse of play is presented as a tool increasingly wielded by the adult in what is termed planned or purposeful play. An incomplete understanding of the intrinsic value of play in more formal early years settings can lead the practitioner in this direction. Problems may arise in settings where the image of play as valuable in itself is perceived less favourably, and therefore play is vulnerable in its position. When discussing practice in some schools, Nutbrown describes how play has been

> castigated and sidelined in favour of . . . 'work' resulting in pressure on Early Years teachers to concentrate on academic learning at the expense of play.

Indeed in response to a parental inquiry about what their child had been playing with today, a year 1 child was heard to remark wearily and with a degree of disbelief, 'Play? We are all about achievement now!'

(2011: 114)

A similar image of play is expressed in Linklater's (2006) study of reception aged children, which indicates that children themselves are aware of the value placed on work and the sidelining of play. In interview the children in his study clearly articulated the Reception classroom as a place where the teacher is in charge and where work, principally based on literacy and numeracy, is valued; play can be engaged in when work is done, free from teacher control, and usually outside. Children themselves can feel that outdoor playtime is the only time they have for 'real' play in school as this reception aged child notes:

Yes we do play at school. We play on the playground. We make families of stones and dress them up with leaves at break time, or we break up leaves and make potions with a stick. The rest of the time it is just work though . . . on Friday we get Golden time, we can play then for a bit.

Is this the picture of play in early years we want to paint? Shouldn't every moment be a golden moment?

Valuing play

Alternative to this rather gloomy vision of the possible state of play, Strandell (2000: 148) proposes play, not as a preparation for life, but as a 'resource for participation in everyday life'. This approach echoes the work of Rogoff (2003) on 'guided participation' in communities, where learning and development is firmly placed within culture and the child's playful activities take place with others in genuine experiences. Similarly in the approach to early years care and education of the preschool and infant-toddler provision of the Reggio Emilia district, and woven within the Te Whāriki curriculum in New Zealand (1996), learning is viewed as being situated among people, places and things. In this image, a child's playful ideas, which explore the boundaries between reality and fantasy, are valued and celebrated and are given due respect and regard. Through the construct of the competent child, play can be foregrounded as a means by which a developing child can participate in the life of the community around him, as a support in his meaning-making, and as purposeful to him. This places the child as central and powerful in his development and learning, and provides a model of play as one of the tools at his disposal, and through which he can explore his curiosities and fascinations, as illustrated in Encounter: Ed and his trains.

Clearly in this setting, due to the sensitive support and provision of the practitioners, Ed was able to explore his particular and single fascination for as long as he needed. Through his play, perhaps viewed as repetitive to an observer, this

---

ENCOUNTER: Ed and his trains

Ed is playing with the train set. He has been playing with this all week, linking bridges together. By Friday he is trying to elevate the track, building it up on wooden bricks. He works with focus and determination, persisting in the face of difficulty and instability. He uses gesture to communicate what he is trying to build . . . a bridge, we think. At home time photographs are shared and mum exclaims 'that's the Ribblehead viaduct! We went there at half term. He loved it'. A meaning is shared, an adventure begins . . .

---

child could be perceived to be seeking to recreate, communicate and make meaning from his experiences. Due to play's complexity and subjectivity it can be hard to interpret objectively and with any certainty. We can only speculate on the purpose and meaning of this play to this child. Observation can reveal it to be chaotic and without apparent direction or purpose, or totally purposeful. Discussion with and shared reflection of these playful activities are crucial between parents and colleagues; however the most important point to note is that *all play* is purposeful and meaningful *to the player*.

Key features of play are identified by Santer *et al.*:

> The essence of play is that it arises from children's innate need to express themselves, to explore, learn about and make sense of their world. Its benefits for children derive from them making their own choices, following their own instincts. At play, children have a certain freedom and autonomy from adult direction. This freedom – to choose, to explore, to associate, to create, to move around, to challenge themselves and others – is an important part of their lives now; and vital to their development.
>
> (2007: 23)

Development as referred to here is more widely encompassing than the aspects of learning of early years guidance documents, and concerns the holistic aspects of children's development, including the positive dispositions and attitudes that Ed demonstrates in such abundance.

Play can be a slow process in which children need time to wallow (Bruce 1991). In other settings would Ed have been able to determinedly pursue his fascination over such a long period? How long before a well-meaning practitioner sought to extend the focus and breadth of his play or to distract with another activity? This is not to suggest that solitary play interests cannot benefit from adult support and an attuned adult will watch, may wait and use subtle ideas to further provoke and extend the child's interests, through observation and skilful planning.

Observing Amy (Encounter: Amy and the seaweed) alerted me to her unease; the planning here involved constructing a means by which she could begin to enjoy the beach more as she already liked the dry sand. It was supported by an

ENCOUNTER: Amy and the seaweed

At 20 months, Amy was experiencing her first beach and I watched as her mum took her down to the waves and the hard, wet sand. Amy looked pretty scared; the large expanse of noisy waves and the gritty, hard and wet sand was not to her liking. She did not want to be put down and pointed back to the dry sand closer to the top of the beach. Her mum was disappointed and I suggested that the next day, we try some activities that would help her enjoy the beach environment more. The next day after some play in the dry sand, I said to them both, 'shall we go and get some water in the bucket?' There was a shallow pool by the side of a groyne and I walked ahead to fill the bucket, pouring the water back into the pool while she walked down. A few buckets pouring from me, and she took the bucket to do this for herself. Her actions were repetitive: fill, sit down, pour water from the near side of the bucket, down her tummy, wait and fill the bucket again, and again and again. . . . The groyne had lots of hanging seaweed and I pulled some off, placing it into her empty bucket; this became a new activity. It was hard to pull away from the wood; she used lots of strength and masses of concentration. Pull, sit, fill; pull, sit fill. I should think about 45 minutes had passed. I suggested to her mum that we wait until she was ready to finish before going back up to the dry sand. We knew when it was *her time* to end the play. She sat down, looked up at us and held her arms out to be carried, back to get dry and warm and ready for tea.

understanding of playful exploration and most children's interest in pouring and filling. It worked because of the child leading *the time for the play*; a crucial element for all children, including the very young ones. They are perfectly capable of letting us know when they are tiring of a game; trouble may start when we begin to dictate the pace.

Play and creativity

In addition to the concept of play as intrinsic to children's development, there is increasing awareness of the concept of play as a vehicle for supporting a particular aspect of development, namely, creativity or divergent thinking. Sylva *et al.* (2004) concluded that children who were allowed to explore materials playfully were better able to solve a problem later using the materials as tools. They concluded that the opportunity to explore materials initially through self-initiated play, without time restraint, possibility of failure, frustrations and stress of meeting a predetermined outcome, allowed children to develop key skills of resilient, independent problem solving. Bruce (2010: 194) evocatively refers to children 'simmering' a new combination of thoughts and ideas in order to produce a 'creation', citing as an example a child's schematic exploration of rotation to create a wrist watch. Kalliala (2006: 22) refers to 'dizzy play', which encompasses not

---

ENCOUNTER: Zak and the worms

In a preschool setting, three children are busy in the sand with plant pots and glittery jelly worms. One younger friend Zak is standing at the sand tray, quietly watching, taking it all in. He has yet to say a word to an adult in the setting. The children, after a great deal of experimentation, collaboration and concentration, have worked out that if you turn the pots upside down and pile up the different sized pots, the worms can be shaken through the holes and emerge at the bottom, to squeals of great delight. After many goes at this the children move on . . . Zak seizes his moment and moves in. In one go he assembles the pots, pushes the worms in at the top but this time he twists the pots round one at a time, aligning the holes, until the worms fall out one by one. A slow satisfied smile creeps across his face, 'My did it!' he exclaims.

---

only the literal physical sensation of spinning round or turning upside down but also the metaphorical concept of the risky 'desire to shake the order'.

In Encounter: Zak and the worms Zak, through his individual problem solving, has shaken the order set by the older boys. From a distance he has been 'simmering', watching, thinking and listening. Being one of the newest and youngest children in the setting, the adults and older children had underestimated Zak: in his play he shows a high level of creative and divergent thinking and a strong sense of pride in his own achievement.

Among some of those authors who consider early years there is an increasing concern to protect this opportunity for children's creative play in the face of what, at times, appears to be an increasing emphasis on adult outcomes to lead children's play. Sir Ken Robinson extends this concern to protect imagination, creativity and divergent thinking to the whole of the English education system. 'Imagination is the source of every form of human achievement. And it's the one thing that I believe we are systematically jeopardising in the way we educate our children and ourselves' (Robinson, 2006: n.p.). He would argue that in the light of the unprecedented pace of technological change and development we, the adults, do not know what the future holds for our children, so cannot prepare them for it. He proposes that the best attribute with which to equip them for an unknown future is the ability to think creatively and access those resources and technology with which they are familiar.

A child's ownership of play

Given freedom to make choices in their play, both indoors and out (Tovey, 2007), children can be seen as powerful leaders of their own learning, supported by other children and by informed adults as play partners. These constructs of children's learning reflect the theories of Vygotsky (1933) and Bruner (1996) who saw play as a source of development and a tool or process through which children make sense of their world in social interaction. The key word here is 'their'. According to Vygotsky (1978), play creates its own zone of proximal development. We can conceive of this as a zone of possibility, a space where children can exercise their imaginations, rehearse new skills, learn to self-regulate their behaviour and emotions and gain a deeper understanding of contexts and roles.

In Encounters: Emma and the Ark, Emma displays a high emotional involvement in her play. She appears to be trying to make meaning out of a situation that has emotionally engaged her and led her to ponder the nature of social and familial relationships. Much later, Emma's Mum recalls that she had been upset at being left with a babysitter only the week before. Considered in this light Emma could be seen to be exploring deeper issues of abandonment, security and parental love and responsibility spontaneously through her play. Whatever our interpretation, Emma clearly owns her play, determining events and outcomes for herself, to her own satisfaction. In this example Mum although watchful and mindful does not intervene, the support of an adult is not needed; Emma is fully absorbed in her play. Santer *et al.* write:

> At play, children have a certain freedom and autonomy from adult direction. This freedom – to choose, to explore, to associate, to create, to move around, to challenge themselves and others – is an important part of their lives now; and vital to their development.
>
> (2007: 23)

Emma can be seen here to exhibit these characteristics in and through her play. Tovey (2007: 119) does not interpret freedom as 'freedom from'; rather proposes 'freedom to'. The latter involves us in a much more engaged approach, not only in removing barriers to children's play but also in actively ensuring children have possibilities and opportunities. This, to Tovey, applies to the physical environment

---

ENCOUNTER: Emma and the Ark

Emma is playing at home. Last night she had Noah's Ark as her bedtime story where she expressed outrage that the mummy and daddy animals just got on the ark leaving their baby animals behind. She is busy lining up the animals two by two on a ramp she has made with a book. She pauses and reorders the animals, this time moving the baby animals from the back of the line to the front so they will 'not get left behind'. The toys are left out, the play resumes the next day. This time the baby animals are put up high on a shelf to keep them dry, and by the end of the day they are safely in-between the mummy and daddy animals. That night at bedtime Emma asks Mum, 'On Saturday when we go out, I want to walk in the middle with you on one side and daddy on the other side and you have to hold my hand.'

provided for children, and in particular to the outdoor environment, but additionally applies to the values, attitudes and pedagogy of the practitioner. This construct of freedom in play again portrays the child as a powerful leader of learning, supported by a perceptive and responsive practitioner. Emma exercises that power as she engages her mother in her plans for Saturday's walk. Santer (2007) refers to freedom and autonomy as vital to children's development. Tickell (2011: 89) extends this concept further to include self-regulation and motivation as essential characteristics for lifelong development, and discusses how the environment we provide must enable them to develop these characteristics. Children are equipped with the intrinsic motivation and curiosity to find out about the world around them, and play is their natural medium through which to do so. They are ready, willing and able, and the type of environment and experiences that we provide, both physical and emotional, is crucial in supporting this desire.

The role of the adult

Whether you can truly plan for play or whether you need to plan for play is a contentious issue in the early years. Smidt (2011) maintains that children's play cannot be planned as this works against the child's freedom of choice and agency. Some practitioners also advocate time and space for children to pursue their own play agendas and to own and direct their own play. Such a view of play could seem anarchic and chaotic in practice in a ninety place nursery. Smidt goes on to suggest that play can be planned for through careful resourcing of the learning environment and the provision of adequate time. The learning environment both indoors and outside can therefore be seen to play a vital role in fostering active, adventurous and challenging play experiences.

Sylva et al. (2004) suggest that a combination of child-led and adult-led activities provide the best outcomes for children. 'Effective' settings are seen to be those that offer a mixture of direct instruction and 'potentially instructive' play activities. In order to achieve this, many settings partition the day into free play, structured play, adult-led focus group activities and large and small group time. This can lead to the fragmentation of the day and can limit time spent on play. Here the adults in the setting are in a position of power, able to decide which activities to prioritise and privilege. Jordan (2009) suggests that approaches that involve the co-construction of learning can empower children as they recognise and build on children's ideas and perspectives. Wood (2010) offers such a model of practice where power is shared between adult and child. The day is reconceptualised as periods of joint activity and guided, playful interaction. Experiences over the day flow along a continuum to avoid the perception of a dichotomy of 'work' and 'play'. Exemplified in practice, focus activities are not exclusively adult-led; rather they are shared episodes rich in sustained shared thinking and offer opportunities for joint wondering, problem solving and reciprocal learning.

Clearly to do this in practice requires careful observation and skilful negotiation in order to maintain a delicate balance of adult suggested and child-led activity.

> ### ENCOUNTER: Pattern making
>
> Kai and Alfie were working in the making area. They said to Sandra, a nearby practitioner, 'we have decided that we want to make you a dress, Kai's mum knows how to make patterns. Can we measure you?'

This is a difficult dance, one that needs to be finely tuned; children do not always readily accept adults as play partners and negotiating the boundary between facilitating play and managing play can present a challenge. We all have experience of intervening in play only to find ourselves suddenly alone, having killed the play through our enthusiasm to be involved and introduce our own agendas. We also must be aware that play that is planned and purposeful in the eyes of the adult and perceived to be a playful experience can cease to be regarded as play by children (Moyles, 2010). However, as Wood suggests above, skilful planning can allow for play that encompasses both the child and adult perspectives. When talking about her kindergarten children Vivian Gussin Paley (2001: 4) states that young children, 'quickly respond to those who keep unravelling the endless possibilities'. When planning for play, the role of the adult is to be playful and interactive, watchful and open to possibilities, to anticipate and respond contingently and to reflect and evaluate in order to enhance provision.

Planning for play should be both flexible and responsive and flow with the needs of children. If rich, authentic and purposeful play possibilities are to be provided, practitioners need to be thoughtful, open minded and observant of children's interests and fascinations (DCSF, 2009 and 2010; DfES, 2007), which can provide the starting point for the planning process, the start of a joint venture. As a head teacher said: 'Let's base our planning for children on what is round the corner.' We need to provide meaningful and relevant experiences for children based on their own contexts and experiences, events in their own lives, in their families and communities. At times the experiences 'round the corner' for our children may differ from our own and reflect different values. If we privilege café role play are we denying the chip shop? If we assume all boys will be interested in pirate play then are we overlooking the boys with different interests?

If we are to be the agents of change for children in our settings, we need to be tuned in to the experiences in their daily lives and seek to provide that which matters most to them in our provision.

The role of the adult in outdoor play

The value of outdoor play would appear to have special and additional significance and possibilities for children's experiences in the early years. Within many children there seems to be a natural drive to play outside, making sense of their world.

Thomas and Harding (2011) suggest that the natural elements control the outdoor environment more than humans ever can, and as a consequence the outdoor environment is less influenced by the practitioners than the indoor; they see the outdoors as a prime environment to support children's developing autonomy and sense-making (see Chapter 4 for further exploration of these ideas). If play in the natural environment can be recognised to contribute to a child's sense of identity and belonging in their world, then we should consider the element of *separatedness* in the planning and construction of many outdoor play provisions. We talk of children making sense of their world, yet their provided outdoor places are separated from the rest of the world, and often bear little resemblance to any natural environment; within settings, groups of children can be separated from each other. This can be through access to different outdoor spaces or access at different times. Alternatively it can be through outdoor play and playtimes in settings that children mix with peers, friends and siblings of different ages from whom they are often separated in their indoor groupings, allowing a community of learners and a socially enriching experience. They find old familiar places and spaces to play in and objects to play with, though perhaps in a new and exciting way.

Lester and Maudsley (2007) review literature to discover that, through free play in the natural environment, children can become connected to their world, appreciate its potential and discover their preferences. This in turn allows them to experience feelings of relatedness and belonging, which last for them into adult life. Their research also evidences the positive effects on well-being and health, both physical and mental, of experiences in tune with the natural world. In contrast, Louv (2005, 2012) warns us of children experiencing a deficit of natural experiences and the importance of time and space in nature when competing virtual experiences are increasingly compelling. Tom, in Encounter: Tom creating a picture, in exploring the possibilities of natural materials in the outside environment, displays a strong sense of connectedness to his nursery carer.

In order to foster creativity and independence and to value agency in children, thought needs to be given to the emotional environment of the setting if child initiated learning is to be facilitated effectively. In order to create an emotional environment that is supportive of play, practitioners need to reflect on their own beliefs and experiences of play (Anning, 1997). If practitioners have a strong theoretical understanding and belief in the value of play they are more able to

ENCOUNTER: Tom creating a picture

Children in a day nursery are playing out in the garden where Tom is absorbed in collecting a pile of greenery left lying around after a gardening session. He selects the pieces he needs, and begins to lay them out on a trampoline next to where a practitioner is lying looking up at the sky with a child beside her. He carefully arranges the blades of grass. When he has finished he gently taps the adult and says proudly, 'I made you a picture, it is you'.

argue for the rights of children to play and work with parents to reach a joint understanding of the importance of play. Practitioners have a duty to work *within* the statutory curriculum and subvert the notion that learning is to be delivered, formulaic and follow a pre-determined sequence. Play is about active, hands-on learning, a child's own construction with or without others to come to an understanding, moving from the proximal to the future space.

Moyles (2010), Smidt (2011) and Broadhead (2010) note the position of power held by practitioners who are able to choose which types of play and learning to privilege. As confident and knowledgeable practitioners convinced of the value of play we are able to choose to privilege those golden moments of play. As a newly qualified practitioner declared:

ENCOUNTER: Practitioner reflection 2

I hold onto my values about play. I know the benefits and possibilities of sand in a tray on the floor. I know that when I let them play with it they are learning, and play makes them feel comfortable in their learning. It is their security, their own unique way of learning. My job can be to plant ideas in their minds, and to help their own ideas to grow.

Provocations

- By what criteria do we, the external adults, make judgements on the value and purposes of children's play?
- What opportunities are there in our settings for the children to lead the play and pursue their own play agendas?
- If play is loud and boisterous, are we challenged by it and interpret it as messing about, or can we embrace its possibilities?
- When a child becomes fascinated by one experience or area of provision do we decide to move him on? Who moved Einstein on when he was puzzling to discover relativity, or asked Van Gogh to paint something different from sunflowers for a change?

References

Anning, A. (1997) *The First Years at School*. Buckingham, UK: OUP.

Broadhead, P. (2010) Cooperative play and learning from nursery to year 1. In: Broadhead, P., Howard, J. and Wood, E. (eds). *Play and Learning in the Early Years* (pp. 43–61). London: Sage.

Bruce, T. (1991) *Time to Play in Early Childhood Education*. London: Hodder & Stoughton.

Bruce, T. (2010) *Early Childhood Education*, 4th edn. London: Hodder.

Bruner, J. S. (1996) *The Culture of Education*. Cambridge, MA: Harvard University Press.

Great Britain DCSF (2009) *Learning Playing Interacting: Good practice in the early years foundation stage*. Nottingham, UK: DCSF Publications.

Great Britain DCSF (2010) *Finding and Exploring Young Children's Fascinations*. Nottingham, UK: DCSF Publications.

Great Britain DfES (2007) *Practice Guidance for the Early Years Foundation Stage*. Nottingham, UK: DCSF Publications.

Groos, K. (1808) *The Play of Animals*. Appleton and Company. Translated by Elizabeth Baldwin (2005). Kessinger Publishing.

Gussin Paley, V. (2001) *The Girl with the Brown Crayon*. New York: Harvard University Press.

Jordan, B. (2009) Scaffolding learning and co-constructing understandings. In: Anning, A., Cullen, J. and Fleer, M. (eds). *Early Childhood Education: Society and culture*. London: Sage.

Kalliala, M. (2006) *Play Culture in a Changing World*. Maidenhead, UK: Open University Press.

Lester, S. and Maudsley, M. (2007) *Play, Naturally: A review of children's natural play*. London: Play England and National Children's Bureau.

Linklater, H. (2006) Listening to learn: Children playing and talking about the reception year of early years education in the UK, *Early Years*, 26(1): 63–78.

Louv, R. (2005) *Last Child in the Woods. Saving our Children from Nature-Deficit Disorder*. North Carolina: Alonquin Books of Chapel Hill.

Louv, R. (2012) *The Nature Principle. Reconnecting with Life in a Virtual Age*. North Carolina: Alonquin Books of Chapel Hill.

Ministry of Education. (1996) *Te Whāriki*. Wellington, NZ: Learning Media.

Moyles, J. (2010) Practitioner reflection on play and playful pedagogies. In: Moyles, J. (ed.) *Thinking about Play; Developing a Reflective Approach* (pp. 13–29). Maidenhead, UK: OUP.

Moyles, J. and Worthington, M. (2011) *Occasional Paper No: 1. The Early Years Foundation Stage Through the Daily Experiences of Children*. TACTYC: Association for the Professional Development of Early Years Educators.

Nutbrown, C. (2011) *Key Concepts in Early Childhood Care and Education*, 2nd edn. London: Sage.

Robinson, K. (2006) *Ken Robinson says schools kill creativity*. Available online at: www.ted.com/talks/ken_robinson_says_schools_kill_creativity.html (accessed 24 May 2012).

Rogoff, B. (2003) *The Cultural Nature of Human Development*. New York: Open University Press.

Santer, J., Griffiths, C. and Goodall, D. (2007) *Free Play in Early Childhood; A Literature Review*. London: Play England and the National Children's Bureau.

Smidt, S. (2011) *Playing to Learn*. Abingdon, UK: Routledge.

Strandell, H. (2000) What is the use of children's play: Preparation or social participation? In: Penn, H. (ed.) *Early Childhood Services; Theory, Policy and Practice* (pp. 147–57). Buckingham, UK: OUP.

Sylva, K., Melhuish, E., Sammons, P., Siraj-Blatchford, I. and Taggart B. (2004) *The Effective Provision of Pre-school Education (EPPE) Project: Final Report*. London: DfES and Institute of Education, University of London.

Thomas, F. and Harding, S. (2011) The role of play: Play outdoors as the medium and mechanism for well-being, learning and development. In: White, J. (ed.). *Outdoor Provision in the Early Years*. London: Sage.

Tickell, C. (2011) *The Early Years: Foundations for Life, Health and Learning*. Available online at: media.education.gov.uk/MediaFiles/B/1/5/%7BB15EFF0D-A4DF-4294-93A1-1E1B88C13F687DTickellreview.pdf (accessed 1 August 2011).

Tovey, H. (2007) *Playing Outdoors: Spaces and places, risk and challenge*. Maidenhead, UK: OUP.

United Nations (1989) Convention on the Rights of the Child. Available online at: www2. ohchr.org/english/law/crc.htmon (accessed 19 March 2012).

Vygotsky, L. S. (1933) Play and its role in the mental development of the child, *Soviet Psychology*, 6. Available online at: www.marxists.org/archive/vygotsky/works/1933/play. htm (accessed 17 August 2011).

Vygotsky, L. S. (1978) *Mind in Society*. Cambridge, MA: Harvard University Press.

Wood, E. (2010) Developing integrated pedagogical approaches to play and learning. In: Broadhead, P., Howard, J. and Wood, E. (eds). *Play and Learning in the Early Years* (pp. 1–97). London: Sage.

7

The possibilities for assessment

Victoria Brown

Mary Jane Drummond has defined assessment as:

> The ways in which, in our everyday practice, we observe children's learning, strive to understand it, and then put our understanding to good use.
>
> (2003: 13)

Assessment is therefore not conceptualised as a product or an event rather as an integrated process of continual and progressive knowing and understanding of children's learning and development leading us to a greater awareness and appreciation of their unique approaches and dispositions to learning. As defined above, assessment is also a process that involves practitioners in reflecting and acting on what they have observed. In effect, assessment should make a difference to the children in our care. As we seek to know and understand children's individual likes and dislikes, their fascinations, their home lives and friendships, children should feel known and valued, that what they choose to do or not to do matters to someone.

Assessment practices are usually categorised as: assessment *of* learning, which is summative, a 'snapshot', used to establish what a child is now able to do following an activity or at the end of a phase of education; or Assessment *for* learning (Black *et al.*, 2002), an on-going process to inform where children are in their learning, and which is used to inform future planning and provision. Hargreaves (2003) proposes instead a continuum of assessment, which is dependent on our image of children as learners. At one end of the spectrum learning is viewed as involving an external body of knowledge to be gained, while at the other end knowledge is believed to be co-constructed with the learner. It is the latter approach that will be considered in this chapter in more detail.

Consider the scenario in Encounter: The magic chocolate pit, which may provoke uncomfortable recollections of our own practice. Here the established procedures in the setting lead the practitioners to miss an authentic opportunity to assess children's mark making through their play. Such a situation could, however, apply to any of us. How often do the structures and systems in place in our settings inhibit what *we do* at the expense of exploring and continuing a potentially rich play theme?

ENCOUNTER: The magic chocolate pit

The playground outside the Foundation Unit is accessible to children throughout the day. The staff have embraced the notion of following children's interests, learning stories and planning for possible directions in children's learning.

For 10–15 minutes Lizzie has criss-crossed the playground many times, filling a small bucket with water from the outside tap and carrying it to the edge of the playground where she poured it out, then poked and stirred with a stick. She was often joined by two, occasionally four other children. They all had sticks. Their body postures and continual movement around the hole suggested a deep level of involvement. They talked about the 'mixture', how wet and sticky it was; the swirls their sticks made. 'What have you made?' I asked. 'A magic chocolate pit.'

I shared this story with the staff in school and asked if they might develop this interest. 'We can't do anything tomorrow, we are assessing tomorrow.' 'Assessing what?' 'Drawing and mark making.'

The value of observational assessment

Observation has a central role in the planning and assessment of learning and development in the early years. Alongside conversation, it is a key way that we collect information about children, which we can use to build a holistic picture of the child so that a child becomes 'known to us' as a unique individual and we can then plan to nurture each child's individual capabilities and interests. Dewey offers the following definition: 'observation is exploration, inquiry for the sake of discovering something previously hidden and unknown' (1933: 193).

In Encounter: Observing Oskar a practitioner reflects on her deepening understanding of the important role observation can having in making known the unknown.

ENCOUNTER: Observing Oskar

Oskar was busy counting the sorting toys. Pen poised, I asked, 'how many toys have you got in that little box?' Oskar took the toys out carefully saying the number names in order but not 1:1. I noted on my pad 'do more counting work' and was just about to walk away when out of the corner of my eye I noticed he had grouped the objects in a pattern. He shouted after me '8! There are 8.' He then did the same for the other boxes '6 here' lining up the objects in two rows of 3, '10 here'. . . . Up to this point I had dismissed his counting ability. I was too quick to see what he couldn't do. I didn't value his capabilities. In fact I hadn't really seen the point of doing observations.

Previously sceptical about the value of observation this practitioner now sees the possibilities and opportunities that can arise from it. It has awakened her curiosity in children's learning and development and has deepened her understanding of children's individual approaches, behaviour, social interactions and views on the world. Subsequent conversations with the parent revealed that Oskar's spatial awareness of number had been fostered during domino games in the pub with his granddad. Observational assessment works hand in hand with a pedagogy based on play. If we are attentive and mindful of children's play, the information we glean through our observations and conversations can be used to reflect on the learning taking place and suggest possibilities for its development and for the development of our own pedagogy.

Observation can be seen to fulfil two key purposes (Rose and Rogers, 2012). It can be used to provide information on children's needs, fascination and capabilities in order to inform planning and provision and communication with families. Crucially it is also a way in which we can gather information, which can be used to reflect on, evaluate and develop our own practice. As we have seen, through her observation of Oskar, this practitioner is forced to confront her own beliefs about the value of observation. Smidt (2005: 33) recognises the importance of 'the search for the significant moment' when observing children. In our practice we strive to capture a moment of magic, a moment of learning or to be able to see the significance of apparently ordinary moments; however, in this encounter, the practitioner has captured a 'significant moment' in her own learning, one she can reflect on, share with others and one she can use to develop her own practice and the practice within the setting. Assessment for learning can, therefore, be a participative and co-constructed process for practitioner and child, between practitioners and for practitioners and parents.

The value of reflective practice

The types of assessments you choose to use depend very much on the purposes of your assessment. If your purpose is to use assessment as a tool to fill in gaps in skills and knowledge then you will naturally turn to approaches that facilitate the filling in of assessment grids or computer-based activity. If your purposes are to find out about what interests children have in order to inspire, excite and provide a meaningful and relevant curriculum, to share and celebrate learning in an accessible and meaningful way with others, then you may turn to observation and other narrative forms of assessment such as learning stories (Carr, 2001) or learning journeys (DfES, 2007). If you are required to set targets and next steps then these too will influence your choice of format and approach. As we will see, what we believe about children, their capabilities, strengths and needs also impacts on our practice and the approaches that we choose to use. Assessment is also very much a part of a wider, political agenda. (see Brown, Moran and Woods in Hawkins, 2016.

Wood (2011) suggests that practitioners need to critically examine their own value and belief systems, which have developed as a result of their personal and professional experiences and the policies and ethos of the settings within which they work. She argues that in doing so practitioners can move beyond simply accepting and implementing policy, becoming, instead, agents of change in their settings, with the ability to challenge and transform policy and practice. Drummond (2003) warns that we cannot just take on other people's values and claim them as our own; we need to actively challenge our beliefs and seek our own meanings within our own contexts. A good starting point for reflection may be to consider and decide 'what to give value to' (Rinaldi, 2006: 70) in assessments. This suggests that adults hold a position of considerable power, able to decide which kind of learning and assessment to privilege (Glazzard *et al.*, 2010), although we recognize the external demands placed on settings. Such a position comes with a moral responsibility to do what is right for children and families, therefore it is vital for practitioners to reflect on and discuss the practices that both they and their children and families really want and value.

This provides an important starting point for reflection and discussion in staff teams. If we start by re-examining our experiences and views on childhood we will be able to confront and challenge our ideas and perceptions and ensure that our practices, including our assessment practices, are in tune with our principles. We need to consider the purpose of our assessments; why and what we assess and who we are doing it for. We then need to consider the best methods to use to collect the information we need and how we will use the information we gain. We need to consider what we learn from our assessments and how it impacts on our practice. In the words of a colleague we should 'assess what we value and value what we assess'. In order to do this we need to stand back and take stock of the approaches we use and the messages they give to the wider community about our values and beliefs. Is this how we wish to be seen? How would we wish to be perceived by others? We need to open our hearts and discuss our feelings and values. In the longer term these values will help us to hold onto the principles we hold dear and to resist the pressures of top-down, objective driven approaches and policies that may not be developmentally appropriate or valuing.

All of us have an image of the child, shaped in part from our own experiences as children but also shaped by the children we are privileged to have met, and by dominant cultural beliefs about what childhood should be. Our image of the child can lead us to take a deficit approach to children's learning and development, seeing children as empty vessels to be filled, as passive recipients of knowledge. Alternatively we can conceptualise the child as an active participant, as a capable and confident learner and take what they know and can do as our starting points.

Nutbrown (2006: 134) considers assessments that fail to take account of the child's unique capabilities as 'disrespectful'; these include teaching informed by targets, ages or stages, teaching based on predetermined teaching objectives and assessment practices contrived in order to audit or track the progress of a cohort. It is easy to see how external pressures can lead to the adoption of inappropriate assessment practices, those that are time efficient, easy to manage and that help tick boxes and fill in children's profiles. As practitioners we may recognise the value and importance of observation and assessment yet may be practically challenged in fitting it all in. It may prove difficult to find a quiet moment to talk to children about their play in a bustling ninety place nursery, to make sense of the mountain of post-it notes produced after a busy day. Some practitioners speak about the pressures on them to meet curriculum demands in order to tick off outcomes achieved, or to set inappropriate targets for children, or to set limits on what children can achieve in order to prove 'value added' later in school. Settings are accountable for the quality of the experience they provide and for their impact on outcomes for children. Under these pressures it can be difficult to move beyond a tick box culture of auditing, target setting and the agenda dictated by Ofsted or school improvement. Practitioners continue to debate and argue all baseline assessments piloted in 2015–16. In one foundation setting a practitioner turned the rich tapestry of information jotted on post-it notes and planned observations into a ticklist as she perceived this to be of more use to the other practitioners when filling in the profile.

We need to be mindful of any summative checks that reduce children's wonderful achievements to something small and ticked. There is significant value in you taking the lead and sharing good assessment practice with other professionals, particularly for 0–2s: this *is* an area of your expertise.

Nutbrown (2006) argues for 'respectful assessment' or 'authentic assessment' (Fiore, 2012); that which is holistic, contextual and values the equal participation of child, parents and educators, working together to record development, progress and achievement. In fact the word 'assessment' is derived from the Latin for 'sit beside' (Wiggins, 1993). Rinaldi (2006: 25) echoes this idea when she talks of the role of the teacher as 'staying by the children's side'. This is a powerful notion; the practitioner sitting beside the child, not in front of, but beside, as an equal partner in learning, observant and on hand.

Respectful and participatory assessment approaches

Article 12 of the United Nations Convention on the Rights of the Child (UN, 1989) and the Children Acts (1989 and 2004) state the necessity of taking children's views into account and have led to a concern to introduce valuing and participatory approaches in children's services, schools and settings nationally. There are a number of influential national and international approaches that view children as competent and confident learners and seek to meaningfully involve young children in assessing and reflecting on their own learning. These build on Vygotskian theory (1933) of children co-constructing learning with more knowledgeable others. The powerful and competent learning recognised by Malaguzzi (1993) throughout our chapters should be met by an equally valuing and empowering form of assessment. Rinaldi (2004: 1) has described documentation and assessment as an 'act of love and interaction'.

In these settings the role of the adult is to be there for the children, to facilitate and to actively listen to children in order to seek their meanings as they engage with the emerging (possible) projects or *progettazione* in the setting. 'Listening as an active verb, [. . .] involves interpretation, giving meaning to the message and value to those who offer it' (Rinaldi, 2006: 65). Practitioner notes, photographs, video and sound recordings all play a part in capturing the 'hundred languages of children' (Malaguzzi, 1998: 3). Documentation is complex and should be comprehensive and is displayed in order to develop and communicate shared meanings between children, educators and parents. In this way learning becomes visible to all; it is used as a reference point to support decision making about the direction of the *progettazione*, children and adults are able to revisit and reflect on the learning taking place (Rinaldi, 2006).

Strongly influenced by the Reggio Emilia approach, the Mosaic approach (Clark and Moss, 2011: 6) recognises children's competencies and combines visual and verbal methods to provide a framework for finding out children's perspectives as 'experts in their own lives'. Strategies used to facilitate the co-construction of learning and meaning include: observation, child conferencing, the use of walking tours and maps, and children's use of cameras and drawing. However Clark *et al.* (2003) warn that practices such as these, which involve and empower children, can actually be perceived by children to be invasive, and intrusive on their inner worlds and personal spaces.

The Early Childhood Curriculum framework of Aotearoa New Zealand, Te Whāriki (Ministry of Education, 1996), promotes an image of children as confident and competent learners, actively involved in the process of learning. Children are not just seen as learners but as people with rights, interests, strengths and needs who are 'ready, willing and able' to make a contribution (Carr, 2001: 9). Te Whāriki describes the purpose of assessment is 'to give useful information about children's learning and development to the adults providing the programme and to children and their families' (Ministry of Education, 1996: 29). Parents are seen to offer a valuable perspective on learning due to their deep understanding of their own children.

Central to children's learning and development is the meaningful involvement of families in curriculum planning, evaluation and decision making. Nuttall (2003: 9) points out that this demonstrates a commitment to the interests of young children and families that is counter to the power relations in many western educational settings where practitioners are seen to wield power, informing parents of their children's progress, and where teachers are seen as the experts in teaching and learning. We must ensure that we strengthen partnerships between parents and work in true partnership with a two-way flow of information as suggested in Chapter 2, and in line with current guidance of sharing our assessments for our two year olds.

Assessment as a transformative experience

Assessment can be seen as transformative, leading to change or able to make a difference to children, families and practitioners. A practitioner shares her thoughts

---

ENCOUNTER: Constructive construction play

Up until then I thought of him as wasting time but as I watched him I began to see what he was learning from being in the construction. He was communicating his thoughts and feelings, making design decisions, testing the possibilities, developing a great deal of technical skill. From that point on I knew I had been wrong to try and move him out of that area, to encourage him to work elsewhere. I started to trust in his capabilities as a learner. He flourished; he taught others how to fix wheels in the outdoor area. He even helped his dad fix the car at the weekend. It was the start of a rich dialogue with home. I had never considered that assessments could help to build relationships or be used to find out about the richness of the home context. It sounds obvious really but I can now see how our learning journeys show parents that you *know* their child, you *notice* them, you *care* about them. It gives everyone a sense of belonging and contribution.

---

about this process and describes how it influenced her future provision and image of an individual child (see Encounter: Constructive construction play).

As this practitioner experiments with using and *sharing* narrative approaches, uncomfortable truths about her practice begin to surface. Has she previously understood and valued children's learning sufficiently? Has she sought parental perspectives before? Does she have a story for each child in her class? Are any of the children 'invisible' to her? In further discussion she sees not only the potential for narrative forms of assessment to impact on future learning through personalized planning and provision but also their role in strengthening relationships and supporting a deeper understanding of children and families. Peters (2009) suggests that narrative approaches also contribute to the child's personal storying about themselves and their relationships with others; they may also contribute to the child's feelings of self-worth. Like all good stories narrative approaches have complex characters, significant plots and a strong sense of audience. They are memorable stories to share, treasure and return to again and again.

Holistic development

In practice in many UK settings there tends to be an emphasis on charting the individual progress of children's learning and development. Such assessment can be seen to partition children's learning and development into physical, social and cognitive domains and disembody learning from the social and cultural context in which it occurs. There is however a movement among early childhood researchers towards recording and evaluating group interactions and social learning (Jordan, 2009). Cowie and Carr (2009) argue that practitioners should use assessments as a socio-cultural tool to capture not just child to child interactions but interactions and exchanges between practitioners and children. They therefore have the purpose of capturing and engaging all parties in feedback and dialogue about learning.

Individual learners cannot be viewed in isolation from the contexts in which they learn. Carr (2001: ix) considers that assessment needs to chart children's relationships with 'people, places and things'. Narrative approaches lend themselves to this as they are situated in a learning context. They also take account of children's learning dispositions or 'habits of mind' (Katz, 1993), such as communication, persistence, co-operation or tolerance, which can give us deeper insights into children as learners. It is not just what children are learning but *how* they are learning and *who* they are learning with that is important.

Building on Rogoff's (1990) concept of a classroom as a 'community of learners', Fleer and Richardson (2009) have developed a model of practice that takes account of the big picture of children's learning. Group observations are analysed using Rogoff's lenses, focused on the individual child, their interpersonal interactions and the cultural context within which learning takes place. Shifting the focus of our lens can support planning for individuals, groups and the wider setting and can lead us to scrutinise provision with an eye for the cultural relevance of our resources, practices and routines within our setting. Building on the Vygostskian (1933) notion of the zone of proximal development it is also proposed that observations should take account of what a child can do with the support of an adult or peer, or as a joint undertaking or consider what a child can do independently. Some settings incorporate these into their assessment sheets under the heading of context: who is the child working with? In Encounter: The stickiness of tape we see a group of children engaged in a joint learning episode. We can focus in on any of the children as individual learners and we can also see what they can achieve together as a group and how this is achieved.

Children's intellectual development should not take priority over other forms of learning. Observations such as this provide us with ample opportunities to observe and assess children holistically so that we know how children are developing not just cognitively but personally, socially, emotionally and linguistically.

Laevers (1994) also notes the central importance of assessing children's wellbeing and involvement. To support practitioners in doing so he has developed the five point Leuven Involvement Scale for Young Children, which is used across Europe and in many UK settings. He argues that before we can start to assess children's learning and development we have to first of all consider their level of emotional wellbeing; that is the degree to which children feel at ease, act spontaneously and show vitality and self-confidence in their environment, therefore highlighting the vital importance of a nurturing emotional environment in meeting not only children's physical needs but also their need for love and affection, their need to feel safe and to have their competence and uniqueness valued. He proposes that observing practitioners need to have a sensitive and empathic awareness of children and an ability 'to put themselves in the position of the child' (1994: 8) in order to be alert to 'signals' such as persistence, concentration, energy, facial expression and posture, which will convey children's level of involvement with an activity. His approach also supports our own assessment and evaluation of the potential of the environment we provide and is explored in depth in Woods (2016).

Glazzard *et al.* (2010) suggest that we also need to consider factors such as children's happiness, the impact of family and wider culture, sleep patterns and preferences for people, places or things. In Encounter: Effie's sleep pattern, practitioners needed to know the information provided by Effie's family in order to meet her needs and to support the strongly established family values. Without this they could have offered an afternoon place, which would have interfered with Effie's need to sleep, which in turn would have impacted on the time she spent with her family in the evening.

The influence of culture on children's lives is significant and should not be overlooked or underestimated. Practitioners need to be aware of children and the cultural context of their homes. This has implications for using culturally appropriate assessment approaches that value and take these cultural influences into account. To exemplify, in one setting an alternative to photographing children

---

ENCOUNTER: The stickiness of tape

Taylor, Beth-Anne and Malachi were in the creating area working on their models. Talk focused around how to fix on the 'robot buttons'. Beth-Anne said she was going to try glue but it dripped all over her model, 'that wasn't good' she said as she went off to wash her hands. Taylor, after observing Beth-Anne's difficulties said she would try tape. After several attempts at cutting, Taylor was having difficulty with the stickiness of the tape. She asked Malachi to cut it for her. He suggested instead, 'why don't I stretch it out and you cut it? Like this . . .' They worked together and cut two pieces. They were really pleased with themselves and went and found the practitioner nearby and told her of their success. 'Hey, watch what we did . . .' Later at sharing time they demonstrated their newly found skill to the class.

ENCOUNTER: Effie's sleep pattern

Effie is cared for by her grandparents while her parents work. She stays up late so she can spend time with them when they come home. She eats with them, socialises with them and goes to bed when they do. There isn't a party that she hasn't been to. She is surrounded by her family and extended family and is at the heart of everything they do. In the morning she is up and dressed and off to preschool. In the afternoon, tired out, she has a long sleep.

---

needed to be found as parents expressed their concerns over safeguarding and some parents also rejected the practice on religious grounds. In another setting with a high number of working parents, practitioners use email and text messaging to communicate to parents. One setting realised they needed to find an alternative to written communication with parents, due to the large number of languages spoken in the community.

Meaningfully involving children in assessment

Katz (1997) argues that young children can and should be involved in self-evaluation and assessment of their own learning and development. In order to do this we need to find meaningful ways to involve children. Many settings use a 'thumbs up if you can do this' approach, smiley or sad face icons, or a traffic light system, where green indicates 'yes I have got this', and red, 'I need help with this'. Such approaches I would argue are superficial and require children to move beyond the pressures exerted by their peer group. During review time in one setting, a child was observed looking sideways at her friend before sticking her thumb up. After looking at the child on the other side of her who just happened to be scratching her ear she rubbed her thumb behind her own ear. Such approaches are also not worthwhile unless sensitively followed up on a one-to-one basis by practitioners.

If we want children to be able to gain life-long skills in self- and peer-evaluation then we need to model what effective feedback consists of. Instead of giving effusive 'empty' praise such as 'great picture, good boy', adults can support children by giving honest feedback that involves and respects children as learners.

The High Scope approach values children as unique learners and takes an active participatory approach to learning. A key part of the approach is the 'Plan–Do–Review' cycle (Epstein, 2008), which acknowledges that young children can be involved in critical thinking and seeks to involve children in the daily planning and review of their learning. As close responsive relationships have been formed between practitioners and children, many opportunities for genuine conversational exchanges occur during the day. Staff use sparing but well chosen, open-ended questions, and active listening: 'Why do you think that?' and 'What will you try next?' to prompt discussion. To promote intrinsic motivation in children, feedback about learning is based on encouragement rather than praise and acknowledges children's learning by making descriptive comments and giving specific feedback: 'I have noticed the way you have used the colours in your picture.' In this way children are not seen as doing things for external rewards, or to seek adult approval. Rather control is shared between adult and child in an environment of mutual respect leading to a shared sense of pride in their achievements.

One of the most meaningful ways of involving children in assessment is to adopt a genuine conversational approach. Such approaches are rich in potential for developing sustained shared thinking. Sustained shared thinking can be seen to occur when 'two or more individuals "work together" in an intellectual way to solve a problem, clarify a concept, evaluate activities, or extend a narrative' (Sylva *et al.*, 2004: vi), as such it provides an excellent opportunity for incorporating children's perceptions of their own learning into assessment. Such an open-ended, exploratory approach involves children in describing, explaining and justifying their thinking to others. Through this process they develop meta-cognition and learn how to learn (Siraj-Blatchford, 2009).

A focus for sustained shared thinking can be found in sharing learning stories and children's portfolios with them and their families. Children can see how their drawings and writing and mark making has increased in skill and control over time. Photographs of significant moments prompt recall of thinking and feelings. Children never tire of reading stories about themselves and hearing about their cleverness.

Documentation of learning for the whole group or class can provide rich opportunities for sharing and reflecting. One setting asks children towards the end of the day what they would like to display on the parent board where parents waiting to pick them up can learn about what the children have been learning, thinking and doing that day. Children choose photographs of models made, paintings and drawings are displayed and captions dictated for the adult to scribe: 'Today we have been talking about if we are all the same.' Sometimes speech bubbles of comments children have said are displayed. Initially an easel, the panel has spread onto the wall behind, all at a level that children can access. Other settings adopt different approaches such as the use of pictorial mind maps, giant scrap books or 'floor books' (Warden, 2012), which children take complete ownership of and use to record thoughts, feelings and ideas through photographs, drawing, mark making and writing, and which can be revisited, shared and celebrated as a group.

In Kasia (see Encounter: Kasia's representation) we have an example of a child self-assessing, developing her understanding of the need for accuracy in her representations and self-correcting until she reaches a solution she is happy with.

Observational approaches naturally lead to the setting of next steps in learning for children. These next steps are most effective when they are shared with children in a way that is accessible and meaningful to children. Continuing the metaphor of a journey, Podmore and Luff (2012) warn that learning journeys can give us a sense of direction but there is a danger in mapping children's next steps in a linear way as it may limit children's opportunities. I am firmly of the belief that we can

---

ENCOUNTER: Kasia's representation

Kasia is trying to draw a picture of a game they have been playing outside. She sings 'Bluebird, bluebird through my window' as she attempts to draw the children standing in a circle – 'that doesn't look right! If I keep drawing it like this, their legs will be in the air. I'll have to have another go.' She thinks for a minute before drawing a series of lines radiating out from a circle. 'There, that's sorted it!' She smiles and nods to herself.

ENCOUNTER: Eden's lyrics

Eden brought her writing to me. We talked about how her next step would be to use capital letters and full stops in her writing tomorrow. The next day she skipped into the setting with a page of her own writing. 'What have you got there, Eden?' She replied, 'Lyrics, I'm going to write the music today.'

---

only set the *possible* next steps for children. If we are observant then children themselves will show us their next steps, as a practitioner recalls in Encounter: Eden's lyrics.

Here Eden cheerfully rejects the next steps planned for her and instead sets her own agenda for her own learning and development. So like Eden we too should take ownership of our practice and be able to resist any pressures that do not fit easily with our values. We need to take the time to reflect and discuss the purposes behind our approaches to assessment and be responsible for making decisions that are right for our own contexts, our own settings, families and children in our care.

Provocations

- What is your image of the child?
- What are the purposes of your assessments?
- What do you give value to in your assessments?
- What do your assessments speak of your values?
- To what extent do your assessments have an impact on the learning of individuals?
- To what extent are we as practitioners seeing assessment as an opportunity to open and strengthen channels of communication with families?
- What are the possibilities of you leading training on good assessment practice with other professionals as a shared learning opportunity?

References

Black, P., Harrison, C., Lee, C., Marshall, B. and Wiliam, D. (2002) *Working Inside the Black Box: Assessment for learning in the classroom*. London: King's College London School of Education.

Brown, V., Moran, M. and Woods, A. (2016) Chapter 3. Children as consumers of early years services. In Hawkins, C. (ed.). *Rethinking Children as Consumers. The Changing Status of Childhood and Young Adulthood*. London: Routledge.

Carr, M. (2001) *Assessment in Early Childhood: Learning stories*. London: Paul Chapman/Sage.

Clark, A., McQuail, S. and Moss, P. (2003) *Exploring the Field of Listening to and Consulting with Young Children*. Nottingham, UK: DfES Publications.

Clark, A. and Moss, P. (2011) *Listening to Young Children: The mosaic approach*, 2nd edn. London: NCB.

Cowie, B. and Carr, M. (2009) The consequences of sociocultural assessment. In: A. Anning, J. Cullen and M. Fleer (eds). *Early Childhood Education: Society and culture* (pp. 105–17). London: Sage.

Dewey, J. (1933) *How We Think. A Restatement of the Relation of Reflective Thinking to the Educative Process*. Boston, MA: Heath.

DfES (2007) *The Early Years Foundation Stage: Principles into practice cards*, Nottingham, UK: DfES Publications.

Drummond, M. J. (2003) *Assessing Children's Learning*. London: David Fulton.

Epstein, A. (2008) Teaching students to think. *Educational Leadership*, 65(5): 38–42. Available online at: http://highscope.org/file/EducationalPrograms/EarlyChildhood/el200802_epstein.pdf (accessed 31 July 2012).

Fiore, L. B. (2012) *Assessment of Young Children: A collaborative approach*. Abingdon, UK: Routledge.

Fleer, M. and Richardson, C. (2009) Cultural-historical assessment: Mapping the transformation of understanding. In: A. Anning, J. Cullen and M. Fleer (eds). *Early Childhood Education: Society and Culture* (pp. 130–45). London: Sage.

Glazzard, J. Chadwick, D., Webster, A. and Percival, J. (2010) *Assessment for Learning in the Early Years Foundation Stage*. London: Sage.

Hargreaves, E. (2003) *Assessment for Learning. Thinking Outside the (Black) Box*. Available online at: http://eprints.ioe.ac.uk/2518/1/Hargreaves2005Assessement213.pdf (accessed 30 July 2012).

Jordan, B. (2009) Scaffolding learning and co-constructing understandings. In: A. Anning, J. Cullen and M. Fleer (eds). *Early Childhood Education: Society and culture* (pp. 39–53). London: Sage.

Katz, L. (1993) *Dispositions: Definitions and implications for early childhood practices*. Eric Digest Urbana, IL: Eric Clearinghouse on Elementary and Early Childhood Education.

Katz, L. (1997) *A Developmental Approach to Assessment of Young Children*. ERIC Digest Urbana, IL: ERIC Clearinghouse on Elementary and Early Childhood Education.

Laevers, F. (1994) *The Leuven Involvement Scale for Young Children*. Belgium: Centre for Experiential Education.

Malaguzzi, L. (1993) For an education based on relationships, *Young Children*, 49(1): 9–12.

Malaguzzi, L. (1998) The hundred languages of children. In: Edwards, C., Gandini, L. and Forman, G. (eds). *The Hundred Languages of Children*. Westport, CT: Ablex.

Ministry of Education (1996) *Te Whāriki*. Wellington, NZ: Learning Matters.

Nutbrown, C. (2006) *Threads of Thinking*, 3rd edn. London: Sage.

Nuttall, J. (2003) *Weaving Te Whāriki*. Wellington: New Zealand Council for Educational Research.

Peters, S. (2009) Responsive reciprocal relationships: The heart of the Te *Whāriki* curriculum. In: T. Papatheodorou and J. Moyles (eds). *Learning Together in the Early Years: Relational pedagogy* (pp. 23–32). London: Routledge.

Podmore, V. and Luff, P. (2012) *Observation: Origins and approaches in early childhood*. Maidenhead, UK: OUP.

Rinaldi, C. (2004) The relationship between documentation and assessment, *The quarterly Periodical of the North American Reggio Emilia alliance*, 11(1): Winter 2004. Available online at: www.reggioalliance.org/downloads/relationship:rinaldi.pdf (accessed 15 July 2012).

Rinaldi, C. (2006) *In Dialogue with Reggio Emilia: Listening, researching and learning*. Abingdon, UK: Routledge.

Rogoff, B. (1990) *Apprenticeship in Thinking: Cognitive development in social context*. New York: Oxford University Press.

Rose, J. and Rogers, S. (2012) *The Role of the Adult in Early Years Settings*. Maidenhead, UK: Open University Press.

Siraj-Blatchford, I. (2009) Conceptualising progression in the pedagogy of play and sustained shared thinking in early childhood education: A Vygotskian perspective, *Educational and Child Psychology*, 26(2) June. Available online at: http://eprints.ioe.ac.uk/6091/1/ SirajBlatchford 2009Conceptualising77.pdf (accessed 31 July 2012).

Smidt, S. (2005) *Observing, Assessing and Planning for Children in the Early Years*. Abingdon, UK: Routledge.

Sylva, K., Melhuish, E., Sammons, P., Siraj-Blatchford, I. and Taggart B. (2004) *The Effective Provision of Pre-school Education Project (EPPE)*. Nottingham, UK: DfES.

The Children Act (1989) (c.41) www.legislation.gov.uk/ukpga/1989/41/contents (accessed 31 July 2012).

The Children Act (2004) (c.31) www.legislation.gov.uk/ukpga/2004/31/contents (accessed 31 July 2012).

UN Convention on the Rights of the Child. (1989) *Article 12*. Available online at www2. ohchr.org/english/law/crc.htm (accessed 31 July 2012).

Vygotsky, L. (1933) Play and its role in the mental development of the child, *Soviet Psychology*, 6. Available online at: www.marxists.org/archive/vygotsky/works/1933/play.htm (accessed 17 August 2011).

Warden, C. (2012) *Talking and Thinking Floorbooks*. Mindstretchers Publications. Available online at: www.mindstretchers.co.uk/product.cfm/product_ID/497/title/Talking-and-Thinking-Floorbook (accessed 28 July 2012).

Wiggins, G. (1993) *Assessing Student Performance: Exploring the purpose and limits of testing.* San Francisco, CA: Jossey-Bass.

Wood, E. (2011) Listening to young children: multiple voices, meanings and understandings. In: A. Paige-Smith and A. Craft (eds). *Developing Reflective Practice in the Early Years* (pp. 100–138). Maidenhead, UK: OUP.

Woods, A. (ed.) (2016) *Examining Levels of Involvement in the Early Years. Engaging with Children's Possibilities.* London: David Fulton.

Leading possibilities

Annie Woods and Lorna Wardle

The previous chapters will have encouraged a number of responses as the authors' intentions have been provocative. They have offered an alternative way of looking at the familiar and everyday activities, approaches, environmental resources and ways of organising a setting through a number of lenses or perspectives, some of which may seem uncomfortable, some challenging and some exciting. To embrace a new way of thinking or approaching a task will always involve experiencing disequilibrium, a gap or difference in what has been known or acted, a new or different understanding, and as adults we, too, have our own 'zone of proximal development' (Vygotsky, 1978) where we need someone or something to push us through a barrier into a new understanding or skill. As lead practitioners, it is your responsibility to both acknowledge this for yourself, and embrace the dispositions of your team when considering or facing a new initiative, strategy or perspective.

Positive dispositions, as with children, will need to be nurtured and this final chapter approaches the questions and challenges you may face, through a dialogic space where Lorna and I, as colleagues, will talk to each other across our professional disciplines, experiences and practices, to engage with you on this continuing journey rather than attempt to reach any kind of destination or answer. That is for you to decide within the context and possibility of your own setting.

By accepting the premise that an early childhood and education workforce is a community of practice (Wenger, 1998), and full of dynamic and shared possibilities, we can start with this question:

How can I encourage a team to consider possibilities and change when there is resistance and constant 'initiative fatigue'?

L.W. As a result of legislation and government initiatives we face forever changing demands and leading a community of practitioners through the pressures of change is challenging. It is not easy and even the most skilled leaders find it difficult. A change leader needs to recognise the symptoms of initiative fatigue where staff members may become disillusioned and resistant to the implementation of change.

It is not uncommon for people to react to change with anxiety, therefore you, as leaders, need to be aware of colleagues' personal concerns or lack of understanding for change. Kubler-Ross (1969) defined five typical stages of human response to change as part of the coping cycle, which is similar to the ways a human copes with personal loss. These stages include denial, anger, bargaining, depression and acceptance, all of which can be de-motivating. Although not everyone will experience all five stages, some will experience the emotional stages in a different order and some will revisit some of the stages more than once. This is no different from the theoretical understanding and processes of a child coping through a process of change, but also reflects the secure, emotional and physiological needs visualised by Maslow (1954), as necessary to be met in order for actualising the potential in all of us. 'If we want people to learn from each other in dynamic, trusting, learning communities we need to consider the interpersonal obstacles to creating them' (Beatty, in Davies, 2007: 124).

Goleman *et al.* (2004) describe how the development of emotional intelligence capabilities can help make visions happen, particularly when a leader has strength in social awareness and relationship management, thus communication is the key both in articulating ideas and responses within yourself and in sharing these ideas with your staff to enable full and shared discussion. This is closely aligned to both intrapersonal intelligence (awareness of self) and interpersonal intelligence (being attuned to others); both crucial for effective leadership.

The successful implementation of a change within an organisation is dependent on the strength of the leadership, the willingness and cooperation of team members, the culture of the organisation and the process of implementing change. It also must reflect a confident conviction based on knowledge, research and understanding. Practitioners should be supported during the process of change through reflection and team collaboration, enabling them to disseminate new ideas and information, thus supporting the idea of collaborative learning. Building capacity for a team to engage in change requires moving from compliance into commitment.

A.W. This sounds a perfect model! A setting that is leaderful (Whalley, 2008) with *everyone* ready, willing and able to take a lead, make a suggestion, embrace the possibility of leading. The steps you as a leader can take include demonstrating the following abilities:

- Identify and articulate collective vision, especially with regard to pedagogy and curriculum.
- Ensure shared understandings, meanings and goals.
- Effective communication.
- Encourage reflection.
- Monitor and assess practice.
- Commitment to ongoing, professional development.

- Build a learning community and team culture.
- Encourage parent and community partnerships.

(Siraj-Blatchford and Manni, 2007: 28)

Leaderful leaders are open to suggestions, demonstrate a willingness to transform practice, consider a range of possibilities offered by experienced and creative colleagues and advisors then *work within the context of the setting to create an enabling environment*. The question to ask oneself is: is there an alternative way of managing staff, practice and external demands to create a different place, ethos, community and one where the everyday demands, forward planning, routine and repetitive activities do not overwhelm the enjoyment and creativity of working with children and their families? This self-reflection then needs to become a regular, collaborative dialogue with colleagues, one that enables *unique staff* and *positive relationships* to be the foundation of team-working.

Robins and Callan (2009: 104) link effective working with your practitioners (and parents) by considering the four themes from the Early Years Foundation Stage:

> Every practitioner is a competent learner who can be resilient, capable, confident and self-assured. Practitioners need to be strong and independent from a base of supportive relationships with colleagues or a key person. The environment plays a key role in supporting and extending practitioners' development and learning. Practitioners develop and learn in different ways and at different rates and all areas of learning and development are equally important and interconnected.

(DfES, 2007)

Often, I have then been asked, but how do I build in the time to engage with my staff team at a collaborative level?

L.W. The day-to-day duties of early years leaders and managers can include financial management, debt collection, human resource management, administration, covering staff absences, playground and kitchen duties, marketing and sale of childcare places to ensure occupancy level. With a huge amount of responsibilities, it is an increasing problem for early years managers to find the time to do everything that is expected of their role. The greatest proportion of a manager's time is spent on either administrative duties or human resource tasks therefore it is not surprising that so many of you feel over stretched and unclear where to find the time to plan and implement new ways of thinking to experiment with new practices.

A.W. You may, alternatively, be a leader within a school-based environment where curriculum, staff, extended facilities, inter-professional meetings, senior management concerns and school improvement take precedence over financial concerns and there appears to be little time and opportunity to take forward plans based on children's interests, diverse community events, family celebrations and spontaneous weather conditions. We recognise that all early years settings have unique pressure points, however experienced you are and whatever environmental constraints you work within, but reflecting on how things can be managed differently may well release time and people to do things more effectively and with richer purpose rather than *just* ensuring that all tasks are accomplished.

L.W. In order for time management to be successful, existing organisational structures need to be reviewed. More often than not early years leaders could manage their time more successfully if they prioritised their work load effectively and delegated some tasks to middle managers such as room leaders and teaching assistants. Good delegation is one of the best ways to build team morale, empower individuals and balance workload. Moving towards a culture of distributing power enables practitioners to develop their skills and knowledge and take ownership of their actions. We know that children need an enabling environment to explore and learn. This is no different for us. Practitioners require support and encouragement to take risks and explore new ways of thinking and practices, just as much as children.

A.W. An enabling environment allows babies and young children *time* to explore and revisit, just as adults need time to adjust to new ways of working. Piaget talked about assimilating new ideas until they can be accommodated into routine actions. Not only do we need to think about time for staff development, but also how far our schedules and routines may disrupt the flow of playful ideas and feelings when a child *is coming to know or be* in their 'zone of proximal development'.

ENCOUNTER: Student as leader

Visiting an independent nursery last week highlighted the value of partnership. A student on placement had been able to suggest innovative and realistic ideas for the baby room to enhance the babies' sensory experiences. These included see-through bottles containing a range of different objects placed in front of a low window to catch the light. The bottles were small enough to handle and replaced an alphabet frieze that was restricting the natural light at crawler level.

The manager was delighted that the placement had given them a 'much needed boost' and 'free in-service development'. Quite often, tutors and students can suggest different ideas based on their own experience or practice, recall of effective settings, articles to look through, as well as increase the number of adults working with the children, which may allow for 'possibility thinking'.

L.W. When you invest and focus on developing your workforce, you can successfully implement effective practices and achieve a quality provision. It is important for early years practitioners to have frequent opportunity for in-depth and active learning that is authentic and useful in day-to-day practice. Team meetings and performance management systems can be a platform for reviewing and evaluating individual team members' understanding of their responsibility, sharing information, exchanging ideas and encouraging individuals to become responsible for their own learning. A leader needs to engage with every single individual in the organisation they manage and together reflect on their intrinsic personal qualities. This will enable each individual to understand their role, function and areas for development. Through doing this, you will liberate individuals to take active roles in their own learning and inspire and create an environment where they can thrive and create a culture of a common vision. This breeds a sense of trust and collaboration across the whole team.

A.W. Performance management is often distrusted and feared; if this is the case, peer observation, joint reflection, open discussion and appraisal do not happen as regularly or constructively as desired. A lead practitioner should have the experience to offer informal feedback, just as we would to positively encourage children – 'that was a great story telling today!' or 'I wonder if taking children a few at a time to wash their hands before lunch rather than forming a queue might be worth a try to see if they are happier playing for a bit longer'; this acknowledges your individual team members and nurtures their intrinsic satisfaction of working with you. Nutbrown (2012: 4.25) recommends that all 'staff are able to learn, reflect on and improve their practice'. This should develop into a healthy attitude towards appraisal where there is a joint discussion of personal, professional and strategic goals and possibilities for the following year and a willingness to engage in staff meeting discussions. If you belong to a network, then you could set up an 'ideas swap' session with a setting similar to yours, and many Centres of Innovation in New Zealand used video observations of children to discuss across settings to consider different pedagogical approaches. Don't forget to encourage those staff on training to share new ideas, *and* that these are seen to be used. McEwan (in Woods, 2016: 85) writes about the role of practitioner engagement and is persuasive.

A project focusing on 'Developing Quality through Leadership' funded by the National Strategies and published in 2007 documents the progress of six settings introducing peer observation. The settings all received training on both reflective practice and peer observation which the senior staff had to cascade back to their teams. The settings were also encouraged to plan time for the observations to take place and sufficient staff child ratios to ensure the running of the setting was not compromised. The impact of introducing the peer observation systems was very beneficial and all six settings continued to use it as part of their practice. They also documented that as a result of the observations the provision was developed, with the project acting as a 'catalyst for change'. There were clear developments and

---

ENCOUNTER: Do we have to do it?

The deputy and I had been on the training for peer observation as part of the EEL and BEEL project we were doing. We discussed it with the staff at a meeting. They were all worried about it and one member of staff asked if she 'had' to do it. We listened to their concerns and tried to address them, we followed it up with training using the EEL and BEEL clips and having a go as a group, which they enjoyed doing because it was safe, it wasn't about them. We observed the adults alongside the children's observations we were doing for the project. At the end of the day we told them what we had done and gave them all their observations to read. They were all really pleased with their outcomes that showed they were using high levels of engagement. From then on they all became involved in carrying out the observations. After the project we discussed the process as a team and they all wanted to keep going with peer observations because they enjoyed them. They found they learnt from watching others and they liked supporting each other, so we embedded it in our supervision and appraisal system.

---

improvements for leaders, staff, children and parents. Considering the impact on staff is particularly valuable. Staff reported:

- Feeling 'empowered' and 'inspired': everyone's contribution is valued.
- Feeling a greater sense of belonging, more ownership of what is happening in their setting.
- Better communication through improved teamwork.
- Greater confidence, especially in planning and understanding next steps for children.
- Improved observational skills.
- Developing their own leadership skills because of greater delegation: 'natural leaders' have emerged.
- More interest shown by staff in training and professional development.
- More involvement in evaluating what they do.
- [Improved] literacy skills.

(National Strategies, 2007)

L.W. Creating an infrastructure in which collaboration is valued builds a shared purpose, helping a community of participation to be developed. Many early years practitioners are still working with a 'done to' culture rather than one of participation. Participative management has meaningful correlations with measures of emotional intelligence. As a first step, host team meetings that enable collective participation to provide your team with the opportunity to engage in joint professional engagement to discuss concepts, potential advantages, problems and creative solutions. To exercise team meetings in such a positive manner you can provide an ethos where all practitioners are shown that they are valued and feel motivated to think differently and take on additional tasks and duties. Again, this pre-empts Nutbrown's (2012: 4.32) recommendation that 'settings will be asked to provide [Ofsted] evidence of how they are supporting staff development and needs, and a description of their programme of CPD and training'.

Managers that use the method of supervisions in addition to staff appraisals tend to nurture and develop their staff team resulting in an improvement of quality to service and better opportunities for children. Change should be carefully managed and well planned to prevent too many demands at one time and successfully enable quality improvement. Leaders and managers who effectively apply a two-way flow of communication with staff at all levels provide a culture of openness and mutual respect, which has a positive impact on staff morale. Communication strategies such as one-to-one discussion, middle manager and year group meetings, room team meetings and whole staff meetings form good foundations to support and develop relationships among the teams within the childcare and foundation rooms, and with other colleagues within the nursery.

ENCOUNTER: Team meetings

A day nursery manager used to use a staff meeting as an opportunity to remind her staff team of certain policies and procedures. She felt this was a suitable method to remind staff members of their expectations. After reflection she realised that she was repeating herself on an ongoing basis, therefore she decided to change her approach and she introduced regular staff meetings and communicated her aims and targets with her team. She provided practitioners the opportunity to share 'their voice'; this led to staff working together in a collaborative and collective manner. After a few staff meetings she noticed her team's high level of discussions and ongoing dialogue between each other to agree mutual aims for the childcare environment. Room seniors and other practitioners led and acted as change agents in certain areas of early years practice. The manager used team meetings to train and develop practitioners' knowledge on certain subjects and assess their knowledge on subjects such as 'safeguarding'. Team meetings became in-house training opportunities and in addition staff consultation processes began to be implemented allowing all staff members to have a voice and feel part of the process of change of practice.

A.W. You may find, however, that if you work in your office for most of your time in the week, or have your head buried in necessary paperwork as a senior leader in school, you will not be able to see, listen and feel the practice your setting is providing; going to play, sit with babies, eat lunch with a key-worker and group of children, grabbing the waterproofs for some puddle splashing and talking through the day's 'shared moments' with colleagues, then the opportunities for *reflection-in-action* or fully developing a community of practice can develop. Modelling, further discussed later in the chapter, is a vital tool for a *newcomer* to become part of an established and assured team.

> The effective leader is one who recognises the inevitability of change and is able to plan for and manage change in such a way that those she leads are a part of the process. Change is best seen as a process rather than an event. The management of the process itself will largely affect the success or failure of implemented change.
>
> (Siraj-Blatchford and Manni, 2007: 15)

This is echoed by Nutbrown who suggests:

> I am most interested in leadership with an advanced understanding of pedagogy – where the leader is working directly with children in the setting, leading by example and supporting the other staff with their practice, encouraging reflection and refinement. While management of the day-to-day running of the setting – staffing, planning, and budgeting – is important, it is too often I hear from highly qualified, talented practitioners that they spend too much time in the office and not enough with the children.
>
> (2012: 5.5)

Rodd (2006) cites Claxton (2002) who regards the development of dispositions for lifelong learning as fundamental for leaders who are responsible for enabling, encouraging and evaluating other people. It might be suggested, therefore, that you need to demonstrate:

- Resilience (ready, willing, able to lock onto learning);
- Resourcefulness (ready, willing and able to learn in different ways);
- Reflectiveness (ready, willing and able to become more strategic); and
- Reciprocity (ready, willing and able to learn alone and with others).

(Rodd, 2006: 37)

Possibility thinking, therefore, starts with you. This is a big ask, but consider the satisfaction and fulfilment of tackling a small step at a time to affect the change you and others deem necessary! Practice the '*what if . . .*' idea or question daily.

How can we create a shared community of practice that appears to have an established hierarchy?

L.W. Nursery managers in hierarchical organisations can find it difficult to implement changes within the nursery they manage. Foundation stage leaders in school also face challenges in defending young children's rights to play, active learning, exploration and time to wallow in their own projects. The organisational structure, methods or systems will often prevent you from being able to implement changes. In these situations, you need to develop a sophisticated and valuable role to motivate and educate others in the need for change and prepare them to be open to it. There is usually a common culture of commitment to improve quality. All adults working within the early years sector have a responsibility for continuous improvement of the provision in which they work to improve outcomes for children. Creative leaders are highly motivated and committed to providing the best opportunities for children and it is their ambition to provide an 'outstanding' service for children and their families. Those in positions of power also need to be encouraged to self-evaluate the provision to improve practice. It is crucial to remind owner, senior managers or head teachers that they too have a responsibility to reflect upon and trust new ways of thinking to sustain and enhance 'outstanding' practice.

The early years sector is forever changing and requires open-mindedness to examine new ideas. A hierarchical structure can often inhibit an organisation's creativity; this may reflect a lack of specialised knowledge and understanding in the case of non-maintained settings, and a 'school readiness' perspective from colleagues trained to work with older children and it is one of your responsibilities to educate those who manage them as well as those they manage. Remind yourself that you were appointed to a lead role. You need to be confident that you have the skill, knowledge and specialised qualifications to sustain and raise the quality of an early years provision. Learn to communicate your vision effectively, showing mutual respect with the aim to at least meet half way. You will need to be prepared to invest the time, energy and patience to be trusted to try things differently; this requires both intra- and interpersonal skills.

ENCOUNTER: Appointing an administrator

Increasing and sustaining the nursery's occupancy levels is a vital part of a day nursery manager's post. The manager was under constant pressure to market the nursery business to ensure regular income. She was responsible for collecting, monitoring and chasing payments from parents. Collecting fees was an ongoing task and challenge taking up a large proportion of her time. The manager recognised that constantly chasing fees was constraining her capacity to focus upon leadership issues.

> She proposed to the nursery owner to appoint an administrator to support payment processes and administrative tasks. After appointing an administrator, the nursery manager had the necessary time to observe and model best practice to her staff team. The manager applies the teaching method of 'modelling' when working in the childcare rooms. She models effective adult–child interaction with the focus of supporting the children's language.

Even as an early years supervisor or manager I can still experience a lack of drive and motivation from time to time. How am I meant to handle this when working in an increasingly challenging environment?

L.W. Teachers, leaders and managers can also lose motivation, drive and self-belief particularly if they are feeling discouraged by organisational or financial pressures. Unfortunately, when leaders lose motivation they may cause the practitioners around them to also become less motivated and negatively affect their behaviour and performance. A 'depressed' culture diminishes possibilities for inspiration, motivation and positive attitudes. Effective leaders portray optimism and those around them respond in a positive manner regardless of their own emotions. Having this level of emotional intelligence is an invaluable quality of an effective leader and is essential for successful leadership.

> The fundamental task of leaders, we argue, is to prime good feelings in those they lead. That occurs when a leader creates resonance – a reservoir of positivity that frees the best in people. At its root, then, the primal job of leadership is emotional.
>
> (Goleman *et al.*, 2004: ix)

It is important, therefore, that you develop the ability to manage your own emotions to enable you to understand and manage those around you. A leader needs to be able to recognise and respond to reactions of emotion without sharing negativity across the team. Try to be consciously aware of when you are feeling oppressed. Although you can't stop your initial feelings you can consciously control your behaviour to determine an outcome. Leaders have a responsibility to and for their team to be able to contain their anxieties and emotions and model positive attitudes towards situations, thereby encouraging others to respond in a positive and professional manner. By self-reflecting on your behaviour traits, you will develop skills and competence in emotional intelligence to support you to maintain excitement and enthusiasm within yourself and those you manage.

A.W. These are challenging skills and responsibilities to manage. As a leader, use mentors and more experienced leaders through 'guided participation' (Rogoff,

2003); they will have had to overcome these primarily intrapersonal traits. They will also have had to adapt, change and improvise when faced with change over time. They will help you to recognise the successful strategies and systems already developed and how to organise your ideas and approaches for a new task. It is important to remain calm, not to react too quickly but to take time to think about all aspects of a new piece of work . . . and involve your team through positive leadership to directly converse regularly and avoid over-use of email. Being leaderful should ensure that when a key leader or member of staff leaves, there is continuity and a willing ability for the team to sustain its vision and approach.

How does modelling effective practice evolve into supervision?

L.W. Section 3:20 of the Early Years Foundation Stage states: Supervision should provide opportunities for staff to:

- discuss any issues – particularly concerning children's development or well-being;
- identify solutions to address issues as they arise; and
- receive coaching to improve their personal effectiveness.

(DFE, 2012)

The manager's and leader's role in practitioners' learning and development has increased. We have moved from identifying practitioner training needs to providing on the job development and learning opportunities; this is also reflected in the increasing model of 'school direct' training. Supervisions provide the opportunity for both the manager and the staff member to discuss and praise performance to ensure that staff feel, and are, valued. An effective supervision provides opportunity for self-reflection, encouraging colleagues to develop their skills, knowledge and behaviours. It is important that staff supervisions are a supportive process and are implemented from the onset of employment, to ensure practitioners have a clear understanding of how the setting operates as well as ensuring they are fully aware of their role and responsibility. In my experience successful induction processes, ongoing supervisions and support help practitioners feel appreciated and motivated. I recommend that leaders and managers organise time for one-to-one meetings with their colleagues at least half-termly to support individual staff members with their learning cycle. Where managers and leaders successfully provide this time to colleagues, practitioners have felt valued and supported. As a result, a reciprocal collaborative learning culture across the whole staff team can be developed. A key aspect to practitioners' continuous professional development of individual staff members is when it involves collaboration between colleagues and effective mentoring and coaching.

Coaching and mentoring is an effective way to boost performance within an early years team. It is critical to be aware that there are fundamental differences between mentoring and coaching. Mentoring is concerned with developing individuals both professional and personally. The mentor is not normally the practitioner's manager, but usually it is a more experienced practitioner with similar functions. 'Newly qualified practitioners starting in their first employment should have mentoring for at least the first six months. If the setting is rated below "Good", this mentoring should come from outside' (Nutbrown, 2012: Recommendation 14). Coaching is an informal approach associated with specific areas of individual professional performance and outcomes. The coach helps individuals to develop by giving them the opportunity to perform a range of tasks and learn from their experiences.

Modelling practice is another powerful learning and development tool to educate practitioners and share knowledge and skills. Modelling an activity while a practitioner observes can easily enable the practitioner to understand how to apply principles into practice. If done effectively, modelling can have a dynamic effect and it can inspire and motivate further learning for individual staff members. Modelling practice can create sustainability of good practice and reduce training costs, as well as providing 'freedom to be innovative and creative according to the needs of the young children they are responsible for' (Nutbrown, 2012: 4.33).

Despite all the challenges and demands on managers' and leaders' time, it is important to allocate time for dialogue, reflection and debriefing as part of the modelling process. These are needed to ensure learning and understanding is apparent to the individual. As managers and leaders dedicated to developing your early years workforce, you must overcome these barriers and provide opportunities that can help improve the skills and knowledge of the team you lead. Modelling practice is perhaps one of the most powerful means of conveying information to your team. We learn not just from what we are told but from watching the actions of others.

ENCOUNTER: Scaffolding practice

A manager models adult/child interaction strategies with the focus on supporting the children's use of language. A practitioner observes the manager modelling a ten-minute interactive story session with a small group of children. Afterwards the manager and practitioner discuss the communication skills employed to encourage the children to talk.

The discussion gave the practitioner an opportunity to participate in a dialogue and actively ask questions about the observation of the activity. This is an effective way to build the practitioner's knowledge of interactive story sessions and develop understanding of skills required when interacting with children. The manager was scaffolding the practitioner's learning through the method of modelling.

ENCOUNTER: Cosy babies

After offering numerous suggestions of practical ideas to create a cosy area in a baby room, the childcare practitioners still hadn't created anything, so I decided to loan some resources and create an area with the practitioners. The following week I arrived with my box of resources and with the practitioners watching I transformed a corner of the room into a cosy lilac area for babies. It took less than fifteen minutes to set up. The practitioners and manager were amazed how quickly the area was created using low cost equipment – an old quilt, lilac blankets, cushions, and a large basket with a variety of purple and lilac textured objects for babies to reach and grab to explore. We then visualised the environment through a child's eyes, laying down in the cosy area to feel how comfortable the space was. We cuddled the soft toys and cushions and had an interesting dialogue about how they made us feel.

Three days later I went back to the nursery to collect my resources and I was 'wowed' by the transformation the practitioners had made to their environment with their own resources. They had created a lilac area with textured blankets and cushions, hanging fabric, soft cuddly teddies, and textured displays at babies' eye level. They talked about how practitioners from other rooms had been donating lilac items from home and how parents had made positive comments. Children are spending time on their own just sitting and cuddling a teddy while others have sat exploring the items in the basket.

Providing practitioners with performance feedback helps individuals understand how they can successfully improve practice and raise quality. Settings with a culture of mutual support and collaboration within its organisation may be reflected as a continuous improvement in practice, and a 360-degree appraisal system is a great tool for encouraging a more open culture. By applying a 360-degree system individuals receive more than one person's perspective on their performance. Individuals self-evaluate their performance and also receive feedback from peers, managers and parents. Traditional appraisal systems can be constraining when completed by managers who do not always witness practitioners in day-to-day practice. The 360-degree appraisal system provides a holistic overview of an individual's strengths, overall performance and development needs. It provides an opportunity for practitioners to reflect on their practice and offers a greater awareness into how different people view individuals as professionals.

Supervision and appraisal takes a member of staff away from the children; we do not have the staff to maintain the correct ratio.

L.W. Those early years settings who provide the resources and opportunity for peer based reviews and interaction develop a community of learners. Providing the right sort of development and learning opportunities for the childcare workforce improves performance and contribution to a quality early years provision. Practitioners with high levels of self-esteem and confidence are more likely to embed self-belief in children.

A.W. For some time, schools have provided time for teachers to complete some of the administrative and planning tasks that are routine. For this to be managed, many schools have employed a member of staff whose role is to maintain the ratio, but not attached to a group of children, room or class; they become a highly valued team-worker and one who is attuned to the needs, interests and routines of the whole setting. Possibilities arise when staff are employed in this role, whether it is full or part time, for mentoring, supporting key worker relationships, linking with teaching assistants and room leaders, liaising with students and looking at the organisation through a different lens. As a lead practitioner, carry out an analysis of the strengths, opportunities and costs of this possible model. Build into this analysis holiday, parental and sickness cover where having an employed, familiar practitioner who knows the setting being able to cover staff for this too, with the likely disadvantages of contacting different supply workers for a day or two, very regularly.

Supervision and mentoring of new staff are an essential part of longer term induction and should engender a real sense of community where a colleague's strengths, areas they wish to develop and continual professional development are an on-going and welcome part of the ethos. Well-established members of staff may find this challenging if it is a system you instigate for the first time and it is well worth using a few staff meetings to explain its purpose. Where you are the supervisor, however, it is important that your staff *know* you are actively listening, and are willing to adapt, accommodate and advocate for alternative views, practice and possibilities. Supervision is not a one way process.

Students, trainees, early years educators and newly qualified teachers are excited about new approaches; this feels risky. How do I ensure that safety is not compromised?

ENCOUNTER: New approach

As a new member of staff, I have been supervised by the deputy manager and during our discussions have asked whether we can try offering more sensory activities with the non-mobile babies. I have been very interested in heuristic play and treasure baskets and would like to give opportunities for the babies to explore materials like sand and water and larger pebbles. I have been told that 'it is not allowed' and would challenge the health and safety guidelines. On the one hand, I am being praised for looking at our practice with a 'new set of eyes', but when supervised, feel that possibilities of change will not be discussed, considered or welcomed. I cannot find any guidance or legislation that says we might not be able to offer sand and water to babies.

L.W. Early Years practitioners often have concerns about the health and safety implications of some of the experiences they offer babies and young children. Health and safety guidance does not suggest that babies and young children cannot play with natural resources such as sand, water, soil and natural artefacts. It is the practitioners' role and responsibility to decide what measures can be put into place to prevent injury and spread of infection while ensuring enriched, valuable learning experiences are still being offered to children. By making sure all staff members are trained in risk assessment and management, we can identify potential hazards for children and work in an environment where risks are considerably reduced and experiences are not excluded.

A.W. This appears to indicate a wider concern and area of interest for lead practitioners. There seems, here, to be a couple of things to consider:

- A plethora of guidance and advice, some statutory, some advisory, some hearsay can be used to both promote and defend a range of practices;

- All staff should be enabled to express their ideas in open discussion and try them out with support/be given an accurate rationale for routines and experiences children may encounter;

- Induction, mentoring and supervision, as part of staff entitlement, allow for professional discussions of this nature; regular sharing of ideas and scrutiny of guidance and legislation *should* distinguish necessary practices with those we might provide with those we avoid because we are reluctant or unable to provide (Chapter 4 considers outdoor play with this perspective);

- Pedagogical reflection is enriching, not argumentative, and should be a natural and key part of the jigsaw of possibilities for your setting. With frequent discussion, you will feel empowered to be assertive when new initiatives and strategies are suggested which may seem to contradict and conflict with what has been established as sound, effective practice in your setting.

- A regular focus on children's observations in staff meetings will ensure children are at the heart of your practice. It will also give everyone the opportunity to skillfully discuss different perspectives (see Encounter: Klaudia's puddle in Chapter 1).

I feel apprehensive about trying some of the approaches suggested by mentors, colleagues and the authors of this book and by articles I read. I am not sure I am confident to challenge models and strategies that have been promoted and practiced, and appear to be accountable to external advisors or inspectors. What if it all goes wrong?

A.W. Our intention in the book was not to scare you! The ideas we have introduced have been promoted and discussed over many years and thread through many early years approaches and international curriculums. What we hope you do is carefully consider perhaps one or two ideas or changes and reflect on the values and beliefs that underpin them as discussed by the authors. This should help you feel more confident to open up conversation with your team and local advisor. It is appropriate not to know all the answers: like children, the fun is the getting to understand through experiment and practice. You could offer for discussion your first ideas as to how to approach change with a phrase like: 'I was wondering if we could . . .' both welcoming and accepting where others have a different perspective. We have all tried activities with children that have defied any outcomes planned; the children probably experience as much if not more fun and achievement, and this can be the same for adults.

It was interesting to read a comment by Cottrell Boyce who, writing after public acclaim following the opening ceremony of London 2012, said:

> Danny [Boyle] created a room where no-one was afraid to speak, no-one had to stick to their own specialism, no-one was afraid of sounding stupid or talking out of turn. He restored to us the people we were before we made career choices – to when we were *just wondering*.
>
> [My italics] (2012)

As leaders and managers, you are not acting alone, and the key is for *shared* practice. In a recent article, Elfer (2012: 135) says that 'managers were expected to resolve any problem or manage any situation. Managers were expected, and often expected of themselves to be omnipotent'. Shared practice is anticipated practice; practice that has the potential for possibility because it has been introduced, discussed and is *ready*. Manning-Morton advocates a space in which participants may:

> engage with the more difficult aspects of children's learning and development and also [to] become experts themselves, including their own darker side. They need to be able to look at their own motivations and understand where they come from and through the knowledge they gain about themselves to better understand and adjust their responses to children.
>
> (2006, cited in Powell and Goouch, 2012: 124)

Planning suggests a definite, but future course of action: this is the goal and these are the steps *we will take*. For us, planning means not planning *for* but having established an ethos, your values and reflective open relationships, the plan *is* working at an outstanding or good level *all the time*. Planning, therefore, is making sure that every child is afforded every possibility to enjoy, find out, share and learn with us, and that all parents are involved, participate and are consulted in conversations and arrangements for their children. For you as leader, this implies that *with you*, your team know why all of the everyday routines, pedagogical approaches and ethos are practised. This will have developed through co-construction, staff development and discussion, problem solving, experimentation and a willingness to suggest, to try and to start again. All staff will be involved in your setting's processes. For us, this is planning. It is the opportunity staff take, the possibilities discussed and the development of an assertive voice when challenged by those external to the setting. A new child, new parents, a placement student, an advisor or an Ofsted inspection will arrive tomorrow; we encourage you to be ready, willing and confidently able to showcase and justify your practice.

Provocations

- How do you encourage colleagues in reflection and dialogue?
- In what ways do you facilitate and differentiate the learning within your staff team? When does learning with others occur?
- How can you help staff overcome barriers to change?
- What opportunities are there in your setting to embrace and inspire staff to take on extra tasks and lead?
- Which encounters in this book will you use to provoke reflection and dialogue?
- When did you last successfully change your routine? Why did you do this and how was it accomplished?
- How can you celebrate and sustain continuous improvement?
- Now you have been implementing regular supervisions, are you doing this in partnership with colleagues? To what extent have staff experienced *their voice* and contributed to their own learning? How far could you go?
- If you could ask any of the authors a question, what would it be?

References

Cottrell Boyce, F. (2012) London 2012: Opening ceremony saw all our mad dreams come true. *The Observer.* 29 July 2012.

Davies, B. (2007) *Developing Sustainable Leadership*, London: Sage.

DFE (2012) *Statutory Framework for the Early Years Foundation Stage*, Cheshire, UK: Department for Education.

DfES (2007) *The Early Years Foundation Stage: Setting the standards for learning, development and care for children from birth to five*, Nottingham, UK: DfES. Available online at www.education.gov.uk/publications/standard/AIIPublications/Page1/DFE-0023-2012, accessed on 5 November 2012.

Elfer, P. (2012) Emotion in nursery work: Work discussion as a model of critical professional reflection. *Early Years*, 32.2 (July): 129–41.

Goleman, D., Boyatzis, R. and McKee, A. (2004) *Primal Leadership: Learning to lead with emotional intelligence*, USA: Harvard Business School Press.

Kubler-Ross, E. (1969) *On Death and Dying*, New York: Macmillan.

Maslow, A. (1954) *Motivation and Personality*, 3rd edn. New York: Harper Row.

McEwan, V. (2016) Chapter 5. The role of practitioner engagement in supporting children's involvement. In Woods, A. (ed.). *Examining Levels of Involvement in the Early Years. Engaging with Children's Possibilities* (pp. 75–90). London: David Fulton.

Nutbrown, C. (2012) *Foundations for Quality. The independent review of early education and childcare qualifications. Final Report.* Available online at: www.education.gov.uk (accessed on 5 November 2012).

Powell, S. and Goouch, K. (2012) Whose hand rocks the cradle? Parallel discourses in the baby room. *Early Years.* 32.2 (July): 113–27.

Robins, A. and Callan, S. (eds) (2009) *Managing Early Years Settings*, London: Sage.

Rodd, J. (2006) *Leadership in Early Childhood*, 3rd edn. Maidenhead, UK: Open University Press.

Rogoff, B. (2003) *The Cultural Nature of Human Development*, Oxford: Oxford University Press.

Siraj-Blatchford, I. and Manni, L. (2007) *Effective Leadership in the Early Years Sector: The ELEYS Study*, London: Institute of Education.

Vygotsky, L. S. (1978) *Mind in Society*, Cambridge, MA: Harvard University Press.

Wenger, E. (1998) *Communities of Practice. Learning, Meaning and Identity*, Cambridge: Cambridge University Press.

Whalley, M. E. (2008) *Leading Practice in Early Years Settings*, Exeter, UK: Learning Matters.

Index